MODERN WORLD CULTURES

Africa South of the Sahara

◆

Australia and the Pacific

◆

East Asia

◆

Europe

◆

Latin America

◆

North Africa and the Middle East

◆

Northern America

◆

Russia and
the Former Soviet Republics

◆

South Asia

◆

Southeast Asia

◆

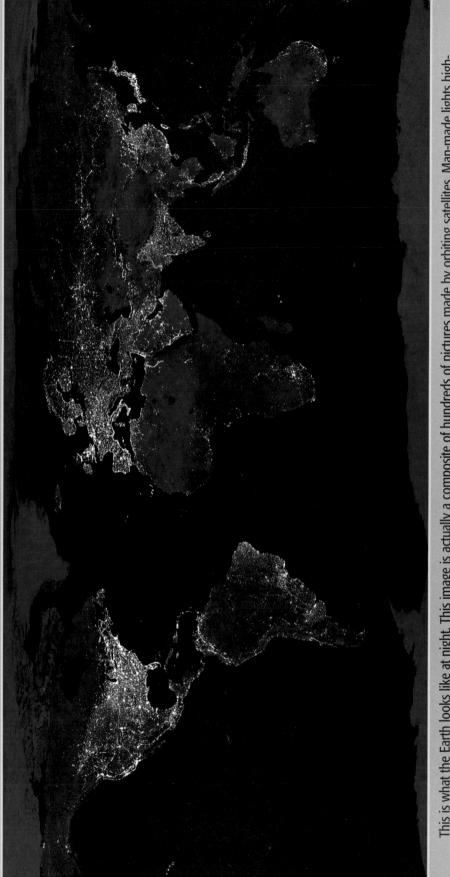

This is what the Earth looks like at night. This image is actually a composite of hundreds of pictures made by orbiting satellites. Man-made lights high-light the developed or populated areas of the Earth's surface. The dark areas include the central part of South America, Africa, Asia, and Australia.

(Credit: C. Mayhew and R. Simmon; NASA/GSFC, NOAA/NGDC, DMSP Digital Archive.)

MODERN WORLD CULTURES

South Asia

Macquarie Regional Library

John S. Benhart

Professor Emeritus
Shippensburg University
of Pennsylvania

George M. Pomeroy

Shippensburg University
of Pennsylvania

Series Consulting Editor
Charles F. Gritzner
South Dakota State University

CHELSEA HOUSE
PUBLISHERS
A Haights Cross Communications Company ®
Philadelphia

Cover: Commuters pass through a busy market street in Kolkata, India

CHELSEA HOUSE PUBLISHERS

VP, NEW PRODUCT DEVELOPMENT Sally Cheney
DIRECTOR OF PRODUCTION Kim Shinners
CREATIVE MANAGER Takeshi Takahashi
MANUFACTURING MANAGER Diann Grasse
PRODUCTION EDITOR Noelle Nardone
PHOTO EDITOR Sarah Bloom

Staff for SOUTH ASIA

EXECUTIVE EDITOR Lee Marcott
EDITORIAL ASSISTANT Joseph Gialanella
DEVELOPMENTAL EDITOR Carol Field
PROJECT MANAGER Michael Henry
SERIES AND COVER DESIGNER Takeshi Takahashi
LAYOUT Maryland Composition Company, Inc.

A Haights Cross Communications ✦ Company ®
http://www.chelseahouse.com

First Printing

10 9 8 7 6 5 4 3 2 1

Library of Congress Cataloging-in-Publication Data

Benhart, John E.
  South Asia / John E. Benhart and George M. Pomeroy.
    p. cm. — (Modern world cultures)
  Includes bibliographical references and index.
  ISBN 0-7910-8147-8 (hard cover)
  1. South Asia—Juvenile literature. I. Pomeroy, George M. II. Title. III. Series.
  DS335.B44 2005
  954—dc22

                                        2005012085

TABLE OF CONTENTS

Charles F. Gritzner

Geography is the key that unlocks the door to the world's won-ders. There are, of course, many ways of viewing the world and its diverse physical and human features. In this series—MODERN WORLD CULTURES—the emphasis is on people and their cultures. As you step through the geographic door into the ten world cultures covered in this series, you will come to better know, understand, and appreciate the world's mosaic of peoples and how they live. You will see how different peoples adapt to, use, and change their natural environments. And you will be amazed at the vast differences in thinking, doing, and living practiced around the world. The MODERN WORLD CULTURES series was developed in response to many requests from librarians and teachers throughout the United States and Canada.

As you begin your reading tour of the world's major cultures, it is important that you understand three terms that are used through-out the series: geography, culture, and region. These words and their meanings are often misunderstood. **Geography** is an age-old way of viewing the varied features of Earth's surface. In fact, it is the oldest of the existing sciences! People have *always* had a need to know about and understand their surroundings. In times past, a people's world was their immediate surroundings; today, our world is global in scope. Events occuring half a world away can and often do have an immediate impact on our lives. If we, either individually or as a nation of peoples, are to be successful in the global community, it is essential that we know and understand our neighbors, regardless of who they are or where they may live.

Geography and history are similar in many ways; both are methodologies—distinct ways of viewing things and events. Historians are concerned with time, or when events happened. Geographers, on the other hand, are concerned with space, or where things are located. In essence, geographers ask: "What is where, why there, and why care?" in regard to various physical and human features of Earth's surface.

Culture has many definitions. For this series and for most geographers and anthropologists, it refers to a people's *way of life*. This means the totality of everything we possess because we are human, such as our ideas, beliefs, and customs, including language, religious beliefs, and all knowledge. Tools and skills also are an important aspect of culture. Different cultures, after all, have different types of technology and levels of technological attainment that they can use in performing various tasks. Finally, culture includes social interactions—the ways different people interact with one another individually and as groups.

Finally, the idea of **region** is one geographers use to organize and analyze geographic information spatially. A region is an area that is set apart from others on the basis of one or more unifying elements. Language, religion, and major types of economic activity are traits that often are used by geographers to separate one region from another. Most geographers, for example, see a cultural division between Northern, or Anglo, America and Latin America. That "line" is usually drawn at the U.S.-Mexico boundary, although there is a broad area of transition and no actual cultural line exists.

The ten culture regions presented in this series have been selected on the basis of their individuality, or uniqueness. As you tour the world's culture realms, you will learn something of their natural environment, history, and way of living. You will also learn about their population and settlement, how they govern themselves, and how they make their living. Finally, you will take a peek into the future in the hope of identifying each region's challenges and prospects. Enjoy your trip!

Charles F. ("Fritz") Gritzner
Department of Geography
South Dakota State University
May 2005

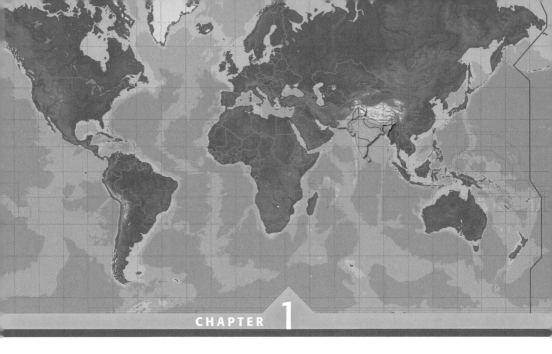

CHAPTER 1

Introducing South Asia

South Asia is a region of breathtaking natural features, colorful and exotic cultural landscapes, and dynamic economic changes. It is a land of physical extremes, including the world's highest and wettest spots. Culturally, few places in the world can match South Asia's rich diversity in ways of life. Languages, religious beliefs, foods, and levels of human well-being vary greatly throughout the region. Sharp differences often occur even between villages separated by only a short distance.

Among the ten culture regions featured in this book series, South Asia ranks second in population to China and the other countries of East Asia. If trends continue, it will soon surpass its East Asian neighbors. The region is undergoing a huge cultural transition as well.

Millions of its people are moving from a traditional, largely self-sufficient folk culture to a modern, urban, popular culture. South Asia has more people living in poverty than any other region, but it also has millions of people entering the middle class and becoming a part of the global economy. The way of life in South Asia sets it apart from the world's other cultural regions, and the geographic region itself comprises incredible diversity and complexity. Here is a sampling of features that make South Asia unique:

- Nepal's Mount Everest, towering 29,035 feet (8,850 meters) above sea level, is the world's highest peak, yet the sprawling lowland formed by the Ganges (Ganga) River at the southern foot of the Himalaya Mountains is among the world's flattest and most featureless plains.
- Cherrapunji, located in eastern India's Assam Hills, is the world's wettest inhabited place, but portions of western India and adjacent Pakistan are lifeless areas of desert and rank among the world's driest places.
- India and its eastern neighbor, Bangladesh, are home to the world's densest concentration of people. If on a globe a person places a thumb on the city of Islamabad in Pakistan and the small finger of the same hand on Dacca in Bangladesh, more than 10 percent of the world's population lives in the area under the palm of that hand! In contrast, there are huge areas of rugged mountains and parched deserts that support no human population.
- No country in the world has a greater number of languages spoken or religions practiced than does India, South Asia's largest country. "Diversity amid unity" is a theme that often is applied when this region of the world is described.
- India remains a dominantly rural country, but it has several cities that rank among the world's largest. In fact, fast-growing Mumbai (formerly Bombay) is expected to

This is one of the mountain scenes en route to Mount Everest, the highest mountain in the world, situated in the Khumbu region of the Himalayas. Reaching 29,035 feet (8,839 meters) above sea level, Mount Everest is twice as high as any peak in the American Rocky Mountains.

reach a population of 26 million within the next 10 years, making it the world's second-largest urban center.

- South Asia is rapidly becoming connected to the global economy. When Americans call for some services, such as car rentals, credit card processing, or computer assistance, they often speak to someone in India! These call centers employ well-educated Indians who are able to compete with Americans for jobs in a new global economy.

- This region is home to the world's largest middle class. Although South Asia has many of the world's poorest people, it also has 300 million people who are well educated and financially secure enough to be included in the economic middle class. This number is equivalent to the population of the entire United States.

- With more than one billion people of voting age, India is the world's largest democratic country. Because of the huge number of voters, elections are conducted in stages, region by region.

- Both India and Pakistan possess nuclear weapons, making them two of the world's small number of (estimated 10 to 12) nuclear powers. A bitter rivalry between these two states has existed for more than 50 years. Because each now possesses these powerful weapons, the tension between them is more dangerous than ever before.

How did South Asia become a culture region? Unique cultures most often develop in areas that are semi-isolated from outside ways of thinking and living. Geographically, South Asia is somewhat isolated from the rest of the world. It is bordered on the west, north, and east by a broad arc of mountains and elsewhere by the sea. Thus, the region possesses not only cultural unity, but it also is a natural physical region that functions as an economic sphere. Given the region's history as a cultural hearth, the massive numbers of people that inhabit it, and its economic potential, this region rivals any other in significance.

Spanning 2,000 miles from east to west and the same from north to south, the region is anchored to the bottom of Asia. South Asia as a landmass is the product of world's greatest collision—the crashing of what is now this region into the rest of Asia millions of years ago. The crumpling of Earth's crust from this great wreck of a "floating" tectonic plate (pieces of Earth's crust) produced the northern rim of mountains that separates the region from the rest of Asia. South Asia, then, is a great landmass bounded by towering mountain ranges and waters of the Indian Ocean. Because of its physical separation, the region often is called a "subcontinent." In fact, the term *subcontinent* is almost always used by the media in reference to this region.

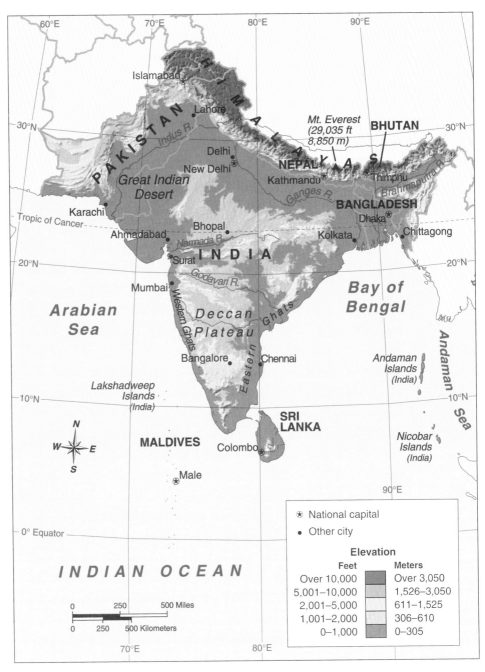

This reference map of South Asia shows the countries, cities, and major landforms of the region. South Asia is a land of physical extremes, including the world's highest peak (Mount Everest), the desert areas of western India, and the world's wettest inhabited spot (Cherrapunji, in northeastern India).

Because *South Asia* identifies the region more specifically, that is the term used by most geographers.

Over thousands of years, while relatively isolated from outside influences, various peoples developed ways of living that today define the South Asian culture realm. In this respect, the region has been compared to a physical and cultural "cul-de-sac." Within this cul-de-sac, a unique and distinct "stew" of diverse cultures has "cooked," or developed. The deep and sometimes hard-to-see cultural roots that unite people in this region are the result of interactions of trade, war, and innovation across thousands of miles and over several millennia.

There are seven countries in South Asia. The largest three dwarf the others in size and population, and one is by far the most populous. India, with one-sixth of the world's population, towers above Pakistan and Bangladesh, both of which have their own large populations. Most of the region's 1.4 billion people live in these three countries. India lies at the center, flanked by Pakistan to the west and Bangladesh to the east. The small countries (from largest to smallest in term of population) of Sri Lanka, Nepal, Bhutan, and the Maldives lie on the periphery. The island nation of Sri Lanka and the archipelago nation of Maldives are both found at the southern edge of the region. Nepal and Bhutan lie along the mountainous northern rim.

At various times, the region's unity has been furthered by political unity. Whether imposed by outside invaders or internal conquerors, this has served to tie the fates of these nations together. As late as 1947, under the colonial rule of the British, the region was for all practical purposes one political entity.

Physical environment can be thought of as a people's life-support system. In the following chapter, you will learn how South Asia's people have adapted to the region's diverse natural environment.

CHAPTER 2

Natural Landscapes

South Asia's unique environment has helped shape the region's culture, economy, and history in a manner distinct from any other setting. The monsoon climate limits when and which crops can be effectively grown. The region's mountain ranges have served as a barrier, bounding empires and impeding the spread of languages and other culture traits, even as the plains have allowed their diffusion. No mountain barrier can rival the towering wall of the Himalayas, and few plains are as extensive and as inviting as that of the Ganges.

With features such the world's highest peak and the wettest place, South Asia has an amazing number of environments. The more superlative features stretch the imagination and boggle the mind. Sitting astride the border of Nepal and China is Mount Everest, the world's tallest mountain, which reaches twice as high as any peak in the American Rocky Mountains. Climbed for the first time in 1953, the peak of Mount Everest rises 29,035 feet (8,839 meters) above sea level. The mountain is so treacherously rugged that, as of the late 1990s, for every six climbers who reached the top, one died in attempting the climb or descent.

Cherrapunji, located in the Assam Hills in far northeastern India, is among the world's wettest inhabited places. It holds records for the greatest rainfall in one year, 1,042 inches (2,647 centimeters), or nearly 87 feet (25.5 meters); the greatest rainfall in five days, 150 inches (381 centimeters); and the most precipitation in one month, 366 inches (930 centimeters) in July 1891. On average, 428 inches (1,087 centimeters) of rain falls each year.

Sprawling below the soaring Himalaya Range is perhaps the world's flattest landscape, the nearly featureless plain of the Ganges (Ganga) River. Between New Delhi and Kolkata, the river, and thus the plain, drops less than one foot per mile (one-third meter).

Lush rain forests, vast expanses of desolate, rain-starved desert, and great areas of moderate temperate climate, along with a cycle of seasons found nowhere else, make South Asia's natural environment one of the most interesting and, in some ways, most challenging in the world. Few regions of the world feature as many different types of physical environments as does South Asia. To describe and explain the variability of these physical features, let us first look at the landforms and the weather and climate. These elements provide the setting for other environmental features and the basis for human settlement and agricultural economy, which are discussed in other chapters.

LANDFORMS

The subcontinent of South Asia is largely composed of three major areas: the Himalayas, the Indo-Gangetic Plain, and the

Deccan Plateau. Sri Lanka and the Maldives are islands that lie to the south of India.

The Himalayas: "Roof of the World"

Straddling the northern part of the subcontinent in a broad arc is a rim of high mountains often referred to as "the roof of the world." The imposing Himalayas form a nearly vertical barrier that extends for almost 1,500 miles (2,400 kilometers). They are joined by several other soaring ranges, including the Hindu Kush, Tien Shan, and Kunlun. These and other mountain ranges were formed by the world's greatest collision. Continental drift theory is the idea that the continents and oceans are composed of plates that float, in a sense, on Earth's surface. Sometimes they move apart, slide against one another, or collide. One huge landmass, the South Asian Plate, is believed to have moved northward, colliding with Asia about 65 million years ago. This collision (which is still happening!) produced buckling and folding of sediments, which created the Himalayas and other mountain ranges. Geologists believe that the collision is still happening, so the Himalayas, including Mount Everest, are actually growing! Compared to many other mountains, these ranges are relatively young; therefore, they are not yet heavily eroded, or worn down.

This formidable mountain barrier stretches from Pakistan through northern India, northern Nepal, northeast India, and Bhutan. The Himalayas and nearby ranges feature the world's 67 highest peaks, making the range a major barrier to trade, cultural exchange, and invasion. Most of these peaks are in India, Nepal, Pakistan, and Bhutan. Almost all of the rest are in China. The isolation provided by the Himalayas and other ranges is an important factor in the development of South Asia's distinct culture. This barrier has protected various cultures from being invaded and overwhelmed by outside influences. Unfortunately, the same inaccessibility allows bandits and terrorists, including Osama bin Laden, to hide there. The

The town of Torkham, Pakistan, sits along the Khyber Pass, near the border of Afghanistan. Towns such as Torkham grew because of the flow of people and goods through the mountain pass.

Tora Bora Mountains, a range within the Himalayas on the border between Afghanistan and Pakistan, is believed to hold several of bin Laden's hideaways.

There are very few passes through these mountains. Where such gaps between peaks do exist, they create avenues for the flow of people and their culture, bringing new ideas and goods. Military invaders also have used the passes. Most famous are the Khyber and Bolan passes. These gaps, along with other, more remote passes, have been important corridors for thousands of years and remain so today for activities both legal and illegal, including the passage of terrorists. Important cities often grow as trade centers at each end of a pass. Kabul, the capital city of Afghanistan, thrived at the western exit of the Khyber Pass, and Peshawar, in Pakistan, grew at the eastern end of the corridor. Kandahar, a city in Afghanistan, located near Bolan Pass, is named after Alexander the Great, a Greek king and soldier whose army passed through there during his drive to conquer northern India early in the fourth century B.C.

The Deccan Plateau

The Deccan Plateau may be thought of as the giant geologic bulldozer that crashed into a mound of earth. It is formed by the smaller South Asian Plate, which collided with the bigger Asian plate. This plateau is made up of extremely old rock and numerous very old, heavily worn mountain ranges. These ancient ranges have been eroded over hundreds of millions of years; therefore, they are not as significant a barrier to people. They are, however, rugged enough to somewhat limit the density of the plateau's population and settlement, and to hinder transportation.

The Deccan Plateau makes up most of what is sometimes called the Deccan Peninsula, the large triangular portion of India that extends southward into the Indian Ocean. Along the edges of this inverted triangle are the two most prominent mountain ranges in this subregion: the relatively low Western and Eastern Ghats. The plateau itself is tilted—slightly higher in the west and sloping toward the east. Most rivers that cross the plateau therefore flow from west to east and empty into the Bay of Bengal.

Flat and Fertile Indo-Gangetic Plains

The vast Indo-Gangetic Plain is sandwiched between the mountains to the north and the Deccan Plateau to the south. This extremely flat area is dominated by the Indus and Ganges (Ganga) rivers. The Indus empties into the Arabian Sea and the Ganges into the Bay of Bengal. When the plate collision occurred, this area buckled slightly downward, causing the area to fill slowly with sediments that washed off the Deccan Plateau and the Himalayas. Here, streams have deposited sediments that are among the world's deepest (more than 1 mile, or 1.62 kilometers) and have produced some of the most fertile agri-

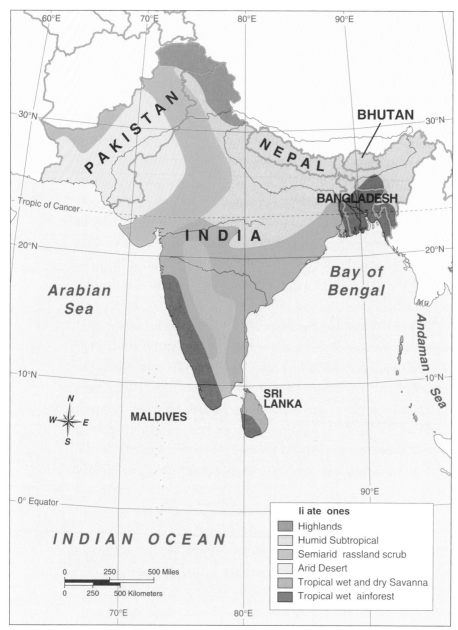

Most geographers identify three seasons in South Asia: the hot and dry, the hot and wet, and the cool. The hot and dry season runs from February to June or July. The heat and humidity build up while conditions remain dry in terms of rainfall. Temperatures can soar to more than 110°F (43°C) in central India. Then, suddenly, the sky "bursts," typically with huge thunderstorms and torrential rain. Gradually, the rains taper off and the cool season arrives.

cultural soils. Because silt is deposited horizontally and incrementally (bit-by-bit), the plain is also one of the flattest places on Earth.

These broad landform regions do not determine where people settle, but they do play a significant role. To an agrarian people, the flat, fertile lands of the Indo-Gangetic Plain, which offer ample water for irrigation, are ideally suited to farming and settlement. Under these conditions, it is easy to see why this area has long been home to one of the world's greatest populations and population densities. Today, more than one billion people—one of every six people on Earth—live in this region, which in area is about one-fourth that of the 48 contiguous United States. The Himalayas cannot sustain large numbers of people because of their rugged features, cold weather, and lack of suitable land and resources to attract settlement and development. The Deccan Plateau, although rugged, does have some areas flat enough and with the right climate conditions to facilitate intense agricultural settlement. Some pockets of land, therefore, have great numbers of people.

WEATHER AND CLIMATE

South Asia is a region of atmospheric extremes. In the far northeast, tucked away in the Assam Hills, is an area that receives record amounts of rainfall. To the west, Pakistan and portions of western India lie on the eastern margin of the world's greatest expanse of parched desert. Such extremes also characterize the annual cycle of precipitation: winter drought followed by the drenching rains of the summer monsoons.

Monsoons: Source of Life; Source of Destruction

Weather refers to the day-to-day atmospheric conditions, whereas climate is the long-term average weather and its seasonality. In much of North America, there are four distinct seasons: spring, summer, fall, and winter. South Asia has what is referred to as a "monsoon climate." Most people think of just

These trucks are stranded on water-logged roads on a highway in Kim village, 143 miles (230 kilometers) south of Ahmedabad, August 4, 2004. Most people think of just the rainy season as monsoon season. In truth, *monsoon* simply means "season," whether wet or dry.

the rainy season as monsoon season. In truth, the word *monsoon* simply means "season," whether wet or dry.

Traditionally, Indians have divided the annual weather cycle into as many as six seasons. Most geographers, however, identify three seasons: the hot and dry, the hot and wet, and the cool. Because the subcontinent covers such a large area, the timing of seasonal changes and their impact varies widely. Some areas, such as southern Pakistan and the Rajasthan Desert, receive very little rain. In the high mountain environments, it is perpetually cold, although snowfall amounts and times differ.

The hot and dry season runs from February to June or July. The heat and humidity build up while conditions remain dry in terms of rainfall. Temperatures can soar to more than 110°F (43°C) in central India. Small dust storms may occur, and many people suffer from dust-related diseases. Heavier soils crack as they dry. In some cases, wealthy people flee to resort cities at higher elevations where temperatures are slightly cooler. These high-elevation vacation areas or resorts are called "hill stations."

The hot season builds until June or July. Then, suddenly, the sky "bursts," typically with huge thunderstorms and torrential rain. The downpour brings much relief and signifies the usually very abrupt change to the wet season. Rain comes in downpours that are frequently interrupted by sunshine. The wet season can sometimes bring catastrophic flooding that causes death and destruction. At the same time, it nearly always brings the water that is necessary for agriculture. The rains sometimes bring disaster, but they always nourish life. A delayed or subdued monsoon season may spell doom for farmers who hope to plant crops.

Gradually, the rains taper off and the cool season arrives. The cool season is cold in a relative sense: Only in the extreme north and mountain areas does it get truly cold. It is a pleasant time of year for both residents and tourists. A jacket or sweater may be needed in the evenings. Soon, February arrives and the entire cycle starts anew.

What Are Hill Stations?

Hill stations are the vacation or resort cities in the mountains to which many people escape during the hot season. These communities have cooler temperatures than do cities located at lower elevations on the nearby plains. This condition results from the *lapse rate,* an atmospheric principle that states that temperatures drop an average of 3.5°F (1.5°C) with each 1,000-foot (305-meter) increase in elevation.

There are more than 80 hill stations in India alone. Those who can afford it often relocate from their lowland city to a hill station during part of the hot season. For example, Kolkata is typically miserably hot and humid during the hot season. It sits just a few feet above sea level. A wealthy Bengali from the city may choose to retreat to Darjeeling, one of the more famous hill stations. Darjeeling sits at an elevation of about 6,000 feet (1,830 meters). Given a normal lapse rate, Darjeeling will be 21°F (about 12°C) cooler. How refreshing! Instead of staying in a place with a daily high temperature that averages 97°F (36°C) during the muggy month of May, one can stay in nearby Darjeeling, with temperatures in the pleasant mid-70s (20s)!

Why Does Cherrapunji Get So Wet?

The extremely high rainfall amounts in Cherrapunji come mostly during the wet season. Cherrapunji's precipitation totals are astronomical because of a combination of monsoons and two other factors, both of which relate to topography. First, Cherrapunji is at the top of a valley that funnels moist air toward the community. A second factor, the orographic effect, also plays a key role.

The orographic effect occurs when moisture-bearing wind encounters a mountain barrier and is forced upslope. As the air rises, it cools. Once its temperature reaches a certain point, the air mass can no longer hold its moisture. Water vapor condenses into water droplets that then fall as rain. This happens on the windward side of a mountain range, and Cherrapunji is located in just such a place.

Other areas on the subcontinent (and around the world) experience great amounts of orographic rainfall. The Western Ghats Mountains in southwestern India also feel the combination of monsoon and orographic rain. With Cherrapunji, though, everything is at the extreme: There is extremely humid air moving into a great funnel (the large valley) and encountering the world's greatest mountain range! The combination of these extremes produces rainfall that is even more extreme!

CLIMATE AND VEGETATION

Climate is a function of temperature, precipitation, and season-ality, and vegetation is one of the best indicators of climate. Deserts, for example, have high temperatures and low precipi-tation year round; desert vegetation, therefore, is composed of xerophytic (drought-resistant) plants that have adapted to arid conditions. Tropical rain forests are another example: They have high temperatures and high rainfall all year round, along with lush, green, fast-growing plants.

Because of the Indian subcontinent's large size, its climate varies tremendously and includes both desert and tropical rain forest. Most of India is either tropical savanna or humid sub-tropical. The southeastern United States is humid subtropical. This climate type has hot, humid summers and mild, humid winters. Savanna climates have a very dry, but warm, winter season and a hot, wet summer season. Along the coastal side of the Western Ghats is tropical rain forest. In the rain shadow (the dry, leeward side of mountains), it is very dry. Another area of tropical rainy climate is Bangladesh and India's far northeast areas. Desert areas are found in Pakistan and along the western edge of India. Grasslands are areas where rain is plentiful enough for grass to grow but not plentiful enough for trees. Grasslands occur in lands that border the deserts of Pakistan and northwestern India. High mountain areas have alpine cli-mates that are too cold for most plant life. On the lower slopes, however, one can find temperate evergreen forests similar to those of the American Pacific Northwest.

NATURAL HAZARDS

South Asia has a number of natural hazards. Through time, some of the world's deadliest natural disasters have struck this densely populated region. Some scientists believe that global warming may cause even more violent destruction in the future.

The region has been hit often by floods and cyclones that come with the wet season. Sometimes these weather events occur together. Cyclones are the Indian Ocean's version of hurricanes or typhoons. The worst disasters occur when a cyclone occurs at a time of high tide. Much of Bangladesh lies at or even below sea level, as do nearby areas of India. Low elevation makes these lands extremely vulnerable to devastating flooding. Several particularly bad storms have struck this area during recent decades. Since the mid-1800s, at least nine storms have each resulted in more than 10,000 deaths in Bangladesh and India. In November 1970, a cyclone struck the head of the Bay of Bengal and caused an estimated 300,000 deaths, most of which were in Bangladesh. This ranks among the world's deadliest natural disasters. Nearly as destructive were storms in April 1991, in which 140,000 perished, and storms that hit the east coast of India in 1977 and 1999 that each left many thousands dead.

If summer monsoon rains do not arrive on schedule, the results can be devastating. Economic losses in this relatively poor region of the world can be catastrophic, and famine can spread hardship and death to millions. More than 1.5 million deaths were caused by the last great drought in India, which occurred in 1965. Nearly 2 million people and millions of cattle perished as a result of drought in 1943. Sadly, the drought-related famine in 1943 was largely preventable, had food aid and its administration been properly undertaken by the British authorities. Instead, callous incompetence prevailed.

In late December 2004, the entire Indian Ocean basin was struck by what many scientists believe is the most widespread natural disaster of all time. An earthquake off the Indonesian island of Sumatra created a tsunami (incorrectly called a "tidal wave") that sent a huge wall of water crashing ashore in many locations. An estimated 50,000 lives were lost in Sri Lanka and at least 10,000 more died along India's east coast. At sea, the

Amid ruins and past glory, faithful Hindu pilgrims gather in Varanasi, India, to begin their day with purification rites on the stepped embankments, called "ghats," along the sacred Ganges River.

tsunami destroyed everything in its wake as it swept across a number of small, low-lying islands.

WATER RESOURCES

Most rivers in South Asia fall into two broad categories: those that flow throughout the year and those that experience seasonal flow. The two largest and most important rivers are the Indus and the Ganges (Ganga). These occupy the Indo-Gangetic Plain and receive their flow not only from monsoon rains but also from snow-melt off the Himalayas and other mountain ranges. With headwaters high in the mountains, they have a reliable supply of water and flow year round. Rivers in the Deccan Plateau, because of the plateau's tilt, flow from west to east and receive their water mostly from monsoon rain runoff. These rivers vary substantially in the volume of their flow. During the wet season they swell, and during the dry season some become a mere trickle while others become completely dry. Where the rivers of the Deccan empty into the ocean, large deltas have formed; these are ideal for intense agricultural use, and very large population concentrations are found in these areas.

In an agricultural society that depends largely on rice as its staple crop, river flow is critical. During the dry season irrigation water may be drawn or diverted from the Indus and the Ganges, as well as their tributaries. In Pakistan and drier parts of India, large-scale irrigation projects with many miles of canals have been constructed. On the Deccan Plateau, irrigation water must be taken from wells more than from rivers because during the dry season, when farmers are most in need of irrigation water, the rivers have less available for use. Tank irrigation is another method of providing water and is common in areas where river flow is irregular. This method involves the draining and ponding of water using ditches and small dams, which store water for use during the dry season.

SOILS

The landforms and climate have worked over thousands of years to produce extremely rich soils along the Ganges and Indus rivers. In fact, these soils are among the world's most fertile. Other areas have soils that are less suitable for agriculture. In mountain areas, soils do not develop because of steep slopes and extensive erosion. In tropical areas, most soil nutrients have been leached, or washed out by heavy rainfall. Desert areas do not have the organic content needed for good agricultural soil.

MINERAL RESOURCES

Abundant mineral resources are found only in India. Rocks in the Deccan Plateau are igneous (volcanic) in origin. This means that there is a greater likelihood of finding gold, silver, and other precious minerals, as well as iron ore, manganese, and other minerals useful to industry. India, then, has a substantial mineral wealth. Because the Himalayas are made of older sediments instead of volcanic rock, they are not a good source of minerals.

Various conditions of the natural environment have helped some cultures retain their traditional ways of life. For example, some tribal peoples and their animistic religious beliefs have been protected by the isolated environments in which they live. The ruggedness of certain areas has served as a refuge for these people and their ideas. As we shall see in the next chapter, the environmental setting has also provided pathways of conquest through which numerous peoples have migrated into South Asia over the centuries as both conquerors and traders.

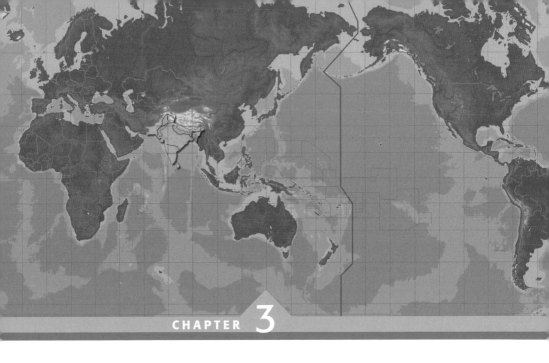

CHAPTER 3

Culture History

Myth, fact, and mystery are often difficult to separate in places where history can be traced back thousands of years. Because South Asia is among the world's oldest civilizations, with a history that stretches back more than 5,000 years, its cultural origins are indeed a rich blend of myth, fact, and mystery. In addition, parts of South Asia, especially the area around Delhi, have been a crossroads for invaders and an exchange point for ideas, languages, and customs. This combination of age and exchange provides South Asia with a rich history and the complex culture that it has today. The mixing of various peoples and ideas over this 5,000-year period leaves South Asia with hundreds of languages, many faiths, and the world's most diverse mix of culture traits—all elements, both material and nonmaterial, that compose a people's way of life. In this chapter, cultural history is broken down into six periods: Prehistoric (before 3000 B.C.); Indus Valley (3000 B.C. to 1500 B.C.); Aryan (1500 B.C. to A.D. 1206); Muslim (1206 to 1757); British (1757 to 1947); and the present postcolonial period (since 1947).

PREHISTORY: EARLIEST PEOPLES IN SOUTH ASIA

Shrouded in prehistory, the earliest peoples were hunters and gatherers who left behind few clues as to their ways of life. These were darker-skinned people and, as far as can be determined, resemble the Aboriginal peoples of present-day Australia. Their technologies were primitive, and their religion was animistic. Their descendants blended with later groups of invading peoples and may be found in the more remote hills and plateaus of India. These people today are referred to as "tribal peoples."

RISE OF CITIES AND CIVILIZATION

In January 2005, archaeologists made a stunning announcement, one that will rewrite the history of civilization if the findings are confirmed. They reported finding the ruins of a huge city at a depth of 120 feet (37 meters) in the Gulf of Cambay north of Mumbai. At the end of the Ice Age, glacial meltwater caused ocean levels to rise, submerging the site beneath the sea. The city dates back an astonishing 9,500 years and covers an area 5 miles (8 kilometers) long and 2 miles (3 kilometers) wide. Scientific investigations here have just begun; however, findings to date suggest that the ruins may be those of the world's first large urban center, predating anything else on the subcontinent by nearly 5,000 years.

Traditionally, based on artifacts found, archaeologists have believed that the earliest permanent settlements in South Asia date back a little more than 5,000 years. It is not known why these flourishing cities were abandoned after 1,500 years. Religious myths that relate to caste origins (discussed in later chapters) may have some connection to this mystery. The earliest

Mohenjo-daro, Pakistan, was one of the earliest permanent settlements in South Asia. Located on the Indus River, it held 30,000 to 40,000 people and had a citadel, an open-air bath, skillfully constructed water tanks, granaries, and drainage and sewer systems.

traces of these urban settlements and civilization are in the Indus Valley. Archaeologists, who study human history and prehistory by excavating ancient sites and examining the remains, have uncovered the cities of Harappa and Mohenjo-daro. Mohenjo-daro was located on the Indus River and Harappa on the Ravi River, which is a tributary of the Indus. Both of these great cities, each with 30,000 to 40,000 people, were probably among the largest, most prosperous in the world at that time. By both land and sea linkages, goods were traded with Mesopotamia (the area around present-day Baghdad, Iraq), which lay to the west. Each city had a citadel (fortress tower), an open-air bath, skillfully constructed water tanks, granaries, and drainage and sewer systems. They even had spacious, well-built homes!

Why, then, were these cities abandoned? Several reasons have been suggested for their decline and, in fact, it may have resulted from a combination of factors. One is climate change. When these cities developed, the region was much wetter, allowing agriculture to prosper. With drier conditions and sometimes prolonged drought, agriculture became more difficult. A second theory is that several invasions by warlike people from the North (the Aryans) killed many people and weakened the society. A third theory is that the cities were destroyed by severe earthquakes and that these tremors also changed the course of the Indus, Ravi, and other rivers. These cities were virtually left to "dry up."

Who were these people and what became of them? Many people in South Asia today, especially the majority of those in southern India and Sri Lanka, may be descendants of the ancient inhabitants of Mohenjo-daro, Harappa, and other Indus Valley cities. These people, referred to as Dravidians, are distinct from other South Asians in language and other culture traits. In racial terms, they are darker skinned and of shorter stature.

Why were these important early cities found here? The origins of any high level of culture can often be understood and explained if one understands three critical terms: *civilization, city,* and *agricultural revolution.* Civilization, defined as an advanced stage of human development where people work and live together in large numbers, shares its origin with the word *city.* Cities serve as centers of civilization. The development of civilization, then, is tied in closely with the rise of cities. The Agricultural Revolution came when people learned how to cultivate plants and to domesticate animals for agricultural purposes instead of simply hunting and gathering. Once people engaged in permanent agriculture and settled in one place, they became better farmers. They eventually became good enough to have a surplus of products. Once extra food was available, some people were free to do things other than farming. They could make crafts, become involved in trade, become builders, or involve themselves in some other specialized field. During their agricultural revolution, the Dravidians in South Asia domesticated zebu cattle, which today are still important livestock animals.

It is thought that development of the earliest cities, such as Mohenjo-daro and Harappa, was the result of an agricultural revolution. This is also thought to have occurred with the cities of ancient Egypt, Mesopotamia, China, Mesoamerica, and the Central Andean region.

ARYAN INVADERS FROM THE NORTH

Routes and passes that today allow the passage of people, goods, and even terrorists from Iran and Afghanistan into Pakistan, India, and the rest of South Asia were also the avenues for people, cultures, and armies in centuries past. The most famous of these are the Khyber and Bolan passes. Included among these invaders was Macedonian Emperor Alexander the Great in 327 B.C. The name of Secunderabad in Afghanistan allegedly originated when Alexander marked this stop along his invasion route. Among the earliest people to move into South Asia through these routes were the Aryans. Originating in what is now Turkey, these pastoral people arrived in the subcontinent in several waves. These new arrivals, who first appeared in South Asia in about 1500 B.C., were better warriors and quickly defeated the Dravidians who were not driven further south.

Travelers in India today are certain to note the general gradation of skin tones from lighter to darker as they travel south. This reflects the origin and influence of the Aryan invasions from 3,500 years earlier. As the Aryans arrived, they further developed the oral traditions of their belief system and impressed this belief system on the people already present. Many of the earliest epics, or religious myths, of Hinduism date to this invasion period, as does the caste system, a system of social stratification that is associated with India. Caste, which is described more fully later in this book, was in part used to justify a hierarchy, or social order, with Aryans at the top and Dravidians below. The term for subcategories of caste is *jati,* meaning "color." This is likely because the Dravidians, who are darker skinned, were ranked lower in the system than the fairer-skinned Aryans.

The Aryan invasion and pushing of the Dravidians southward explains many of today's broader patterns of language and culture that generally coincide with the geographic distribution of skin color. Dravidian languages are still spoken in South India and Sri Lanka. Hindi languages, which are drawn from the same roots as English and many other European languages, are prevalent throughout the northern portions of the subcontinent. Language patterns remained resistant in the southern reaches of the Deccan Peninsula, but the religious dominance of Hinduism permeated all of India. Why the religious dominance occurred across the region when the linguistic domination did not remains a mystery.

Each wave of Aryan invaders made a transition from pastoral nomadism to sedentary agriculture. Pastoral nomadism is characterized by herding cattle, sheep, or other animals without a fixed settlement area. People make their living from what the animals provide, especially with regard to food. Sedentary agriculture is permanent settlement in an area with the growing of crops for food. Later, as the newly arrived Aryans settled and mixed with the local people, some ideas of the Dravidians were incorporated into the Aryan belief system. This unique blend provides the basis for Hinduism, the dominant faith of South Asia today.

ERA OF THE GREAT HINDU KINGDOMS
A number of kingdoms, including the Mauryan and Gupta empires, were organized during the 15 centuries after the Aryans had established themselves in the region. At the same time, Hinduism became entrenched as the region's leading faith. The most famous of the Hindu dynasties, the Mauryan Empire, had

the greatest legacy. It was established in 322 B.C. and lasted 170 years, during which political rule over nearly all of South Asia was consolidated. This period of uniform political and administrative control amid a flourishing economy helped establish much of the cultural unity that defines the region today.

The most famous of Mauryan rulers was the Emperor Asoka, who ruled from 269 to 232 B.C. He converted to Buddhism during his rule and made it the state religion. To record his message and his rule over his domain, a number of sandstone pillars were erected; many of these historic artifacts remain. As a result of Asoka's strong support of Buddhism and his desire to spread the religion, Hinduism's status as the leading faith was threatened. Gradually, however, many aspects of Buddhism were incorporated or absorbed into Hinduism, and Hinduism reclaimed its overwhelming dominance. Many Indian men today are named Ashok, which indicates the reverence that Asoka's name still holds, as well as his long-lasting influence on the region.

A number of kingdoms and empires appeared during the five centuries after the collapse of the Mauryan Empire and before the rise of the Guptas. The Gupta Empire (A.D. 320–550) proved to be a golden age, as arts, architecture, law, literature, science, and trade all flourished. Many of the cultural traditions adopted in South Asia developed during this and the earlier Mauryan period. Many of these diffused to Europe and other regions and provided the basis for much scientific discovery. To illustrate, when you look at the page numbers of this book, you are viewing one contribution: This numeral system was developed during the Mauryan period. Among many contributions to mathematics, the value of pi was calculated to the fourth decimal place (3.1416), and the length of the solar year was calculated to 365.358605 days. Under the Gupta Empire, the cultural uniformity of the region was further reinforced; this is what gives South Asia the common cultural heritage that dates from this age.

No trip to India would be complete without a visit to the Taj Mahal, built as a mausoleum in the 1600s. It was built by Shah Jahan for his most beloved wife.

THE MOGUL EMPIRE

Islam was founded in Saudi Arabia in A.D. 622 by the Prophet Muhammad, and rapidly spread westward across most of North Africa and eastward toward South Asia. Less than a century later, Muslims (people who practice Islam) occupied parts of what is now Pakistan. Various invasions into northern India by Muslim groups from central Asia, including Afghanistan, eventually led to the establishment of long-lasting Muslim rule over the northern half of South Asia. Several series of kings (or dynasties) ruled as sultans. The more powerful kings pushed their armies farther south, nearly to the tip of the subcontinent, thereby conquering almost the entire region of South Asia. At other times, regional Hindu kingdoms prospered, often pushing back the spreading Islamic empires.

The most powerful of the Islamic dynasties was the Moguls. For 200 years beginning in 1526, with the capital in Delhi, the Moguls expanded their rule over the region. Several of the Mogul emperors are remembered today as having made great contributions to Indian culture and society. Others are remembered for their cruelty and brutality. The Taj Mahal, one of the world's most beautiful and recognizable structures, is perhaps the finest existing example of Islamic architecture. It is a tomb built by Shah Jahan for his most beloved wife. Shah Jahan's son, Aurangzeb, the most ruthless and religiously fanatical of the Moguls, overthrew his father and imprisoned him in a cell that allowed him to view the Taj Mahal for the remainder of his life. This brutal ruler seized power in 1659 and expanded his empire in area. In doing so, he weakened it through overexpansion and high taxation imposed on Hindus. His seizure of power was particularly frightful, because it involved warring with, capturing, and beheading two of his own brothers!

Over time, the Mogul Empire weakened, and the area it controlled slowly withered until the mid-1800s, when regional Hindu kingdoms reclaimed some power. As the power of the Moguls receded, however, a new power emerged that would soon come to dominate South Asia as had no other before.

BRITISH COLONIZATION

British influence in South Asia lasted several centuries, including nearly a century of direct colonial rule. Was that rule beneficial or harmful? A half-century has passed since most countries of the region gained independence, and this is still a hotly debated topic. Even its mention evokes anger among many.

Those who argue that it was beneficial say that the British provided a good administrative framework, a model educational system, and a well-established physical infrastructure that includes an integrated rail network and numerous irrigation projects. Others disagree, saying that British rule was harmful. They say that India's resources were plundered and argue that the administrative framework merely organized this exploitation. They also believe that the rail and canal networks facilitated the theft of these resources instead of connecting the country. There is an argument that the rail network was built not to help British India but to make sure that the British army and other security forces could quickly move to pacify rebels across the country. The educational institutions served only to train Indians to serve as cogs in the British-controlled system. That is, the Indians would be underlings in what some believe was the robbery of their own country.

European Encounter

European contact with South Asia began in 1498, when Portuguese explorer Vasco da Gama rounded Africa at Cape Horn and made his way across the Indian Ocean to the tip of South Asia. During the next 150 years, Portuguese, Spanish, Dutch, French, and English traders slowly joined the many Arab, Hindu, and Chinese sailors doing the same. Portugal's first trading-post landholding in South Asia was the small colony of Goa. This remote outpost was occupied by the Portuguese until it was claimed by India in 1962.

Economic competition and the potential for huge profits lured traders to this exotic land. Although Vasco da Gama purchased poor-quality cinnamon and ginger, his first trip resulted in a 3,000 percent profit! The competition was brutal, with conflicts among various trading parties often having morbid results. During his second trip to India in 1502, da Gama avenged the earlier slaughter of Portuguese traders by chopping off the ears, noses, and hands of 800 Muslim sailors.

The British first started trading (and raiding) in the early 1600s. Queen Elizabeth I had given favored merchants a monopoly over trade with South Asia. These merchants organized themselves as the British East India Company; they held a monopoly until 1857. Established in the mid to late 1600s, the first permanent British trading posts became India's biggest cities. Madras

(Chennai), Bombay (Mumbai), and Calcutta (Kolkata) experienced considerable growth as early British trading centers. Over time, the British expanded their trade network from these early bases.

At this time, the French also were establishing trading posts in South Asia. The French learned to collaborate with many of the regional kingdoms and became skilled in taking advantage of local rivalries and jealousies between kings, often using bribes to pit one local ruler against the other. The British, under the cunning and treacherous leadership of Robert Clive, perfected the "divide and rule" strategy learned from the French. By 1765, using this technique, they had established themselves as rulers over several large regions in the eastern half of South Asia.

Consolidation of British Power

From 1765 to 1857, British activities expanded throughout South Asia. Some areas were controlled directly by the British, but most were controlled indirectly. Indirect control occurred as local princes and kings became puppets of the British. The British used a combination of methods including military support, military threats, and profitable trading relations. They also took advantage of local rivalries, used bribes, and even involved *sepoys* (hired mercenaries) in order to secure control over the region.

In 1857, India became a British colony. Profit was the main motive behind the colonization. The British established a lucrative and rewarding set of trading relations. Goods that could be exported to other parts of the world, such as tea and cotton, now often replaced food crops. These relations exploited the local populations and contributed to conditions that left local people, who were mostly farmers, more vulnerable to crop failures and resulting famine. To make matters worse, burdensome land taxes were imposed to pay for the administration of the unequal trade relationships!

Over time, resentment over the unequal trade relationships built up throughout the diverse groups in British India. On top of the exploitation, colonial authorities showed amazing disrespect to both Muslims and Hindus. Temples, mosques, and shrines were misused, and religious practices were insulted. The flash point was reached when army forces were issued ammunition cartridges greased with pork and beef fat. This violated the religious practices of Hindus, who venerate cows, and Muslims, who consider pork unclean, and triggered an uncoordinated revolt across most of north India that threatened to spread through all of South Asia. The revolt was barely put down by rapid and severe military action and was followed by vicious retribution. In some cases, rebels were tied to cannons that were then fired. This rebellion, fomerly called the Sepoy Rebellion, is now recognized as India's first war for independence.

The British Raj

The rebellion of 1857 prompted radical changes in rule over India. First, the British government took more direct control over the colony. Also, the nature of the trade relationship changed as the Industrial Revolution demanded raw materials from across the world. Beginning in the second half of the nineteenth century, South Asia supplied cotton, tea, jute (for rope making), and other raw materials that were often shipped to Britain. These materials were then manufactured into higher-value goods and sold back to India. This unbalanced relationship obviously worked to the colonial power's advantage.

To facilitate the extraction of goods, a vast system of railways was constructed, and canal systems for irrigation were developed to improve agricultural yields. An educational system modeled after that of Britain was established to train natives in public administration and other useful tasks. These contributions provided some advantages after independence was achieved, but for a century they served only to take enormous amounts of wealth from the country. Because most of this system of "industrial colonialism" was set up for the benefit of the colonial masters, it was not as useful in building up the countries of South Asia after independence.

During colonial rule or the era of the British "Raj" (rule), the Europeans often cast themselves as superior, and so South Asians rarely occupied any positions of authority. In many cases, South Asians were segregated from British residential areas within their own land. In one of the hill stations, signs that stated "No Indians allowed" could be found in the so-called public areas of the town! With this official second-class treatment and the exploitative trade relationships, Indian leaders began to agitate for independence.

GAINING INDEPENDENCE

Public support for independence, with the leadership of Mahatma Gandhi and others in India, gradually grew in strength. The peoples of South Asia became increasingly impatient with British rule and mistreatment. In the years before independence, South Asians pressed Britain to "quit India" so that India could have *swaraj,* meaning "self-rule." Recognizing the inevitable, the British hurriedly left South Asia in disarray in 1947. The messy and poorly planned withdrawal led to immediate bloodshed, as the groups of people they had played against one another for more than two centuries began to protest, riot, and fight. Nonetheless, on August 15, 1947, Pakistan and India gained independence from British colonial rule. Sri Lanka's independence came less than six months later, on February 4, 1948. Nepal, although heavily influenced by the British, was technically independent throughout the colonial period.

CHAPTER 4

Population and Settlement

Only East Asia has a higher population than South Asia. South Asia will soon have more people, however, because the population of India is projected to surpass that of China within several decades. As noted in the introduction, approximately 625 million people live in the lowland plains between northern Pakistan and Bangladesh. This figure amounts to 10 percent of the world's population—living in an area roughly the size of Texas and New Mexico! In addition to the enormous number of people, there are huge rural population densities, gargantuan megacities, and other interesting population conditions. The population characteristics of South Asia can be discussed in terms of totals, births, deaths, growth, and urbanization.

Pedestrians and vehicles crowd a street that cuts through a bazaar area in Old Delhi, between the Red Fort and Jama Masjid, India's largest mosque. In India's big cities, congestion is to be expected.

In addition, attention can be given to quality of life indicators such as life expectancy, infant mortality, and health measures.

OVERALL POPULATION

South Asia's total population is about 1.4 billion. India has a little more than one billion. It ranks second, behind China, in total population. When the total surpassed one billion, many in India celebrated it as a great achievement. Pakistan and Bangladesh have about 162 million and 145 million people, respectively, ranking them seventh and eighth among the world's countries. Much farther down the list are Nepal, with approximately 25 million, and Sri Lanka, at 20 million. The Maldives and Bhutan, with only 300,000 persons and perhaps one million, respectively, are statistically too small to compare with the larger countries. If the 1.4 billion does not seem high enough, consider that the current rate of growth for each of these countries will add 900 million more in the next 45 years! India is projected to have 1.6 billion people by the year 2050.

Overpopulation is an obvious problem in South Asia. The population burden on the land is immense. This burden is often indicated as the "physiologic density," the number of people living on a specified area of agriculturally productive land, such as a square mile. India has a physiologic density of 1,688 people per square mile (1,050 per square kilometer). In Bangladesh, it is an incredible 3,800 people per square mile (2,356 per square kilometer)! Bangladesh has nearly 150 million people (half the population of the United States) squeezed into an area the size of Wisconsin. Overall, South Asia covers about 3 percent of the planet's surface area but supports 22 percent of the population.

Population growth is threatening to outstrip resources in South Asia. Growth is a function of births minus deaths. In South Asia, for every 1,000 people, 25 are born and eight die each year. This means that for every 1,000 people in the region, another 17 are added every year. This is a 1.7 percent rate of increase. For a bank account, this is a poor rate of return, but for a poor country, it is a tremendous growth rate!

Birth Rates and Death Rates

The birth rate is a rough measure of fertility. Fertility rate, which is the average number of children a woman may be expected to have in her lifetime, is another measure. In India, the fertility rate is 3.1, meaning that a woman entering maturity today will likely have three children in her lifetime. Just a generation ago, that rate was nearly six children per woman! As the country becomes more wealthy and urban and more women become educated, families have fewer and fewer children. This is very similar to what happened in the United States and other developed countries during the past 200 years.

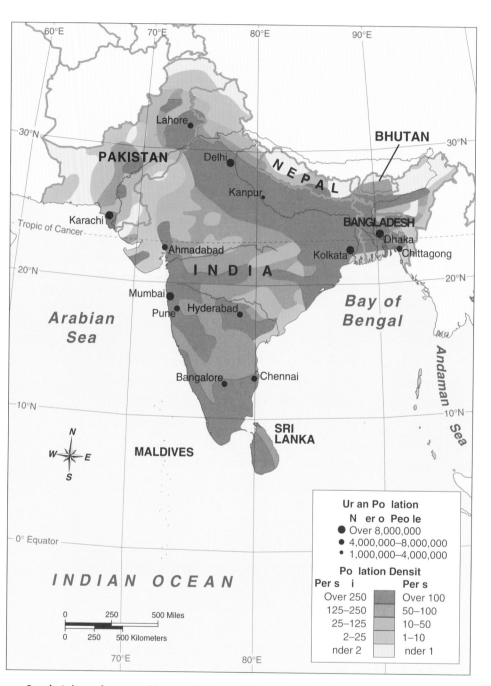

South Asia ranks second in population to China and the other countries of East Asia. (About 10 percent of the world's population can be found in the lowland plains between northern Pakistan and Bangladesh!) If trends continue, it will soon surpass its East Asian neighbors. The region is undergoing a huge cultural transition as well. Millions of its people are moving from a traditional, largely self-sufficient, folk culture to a modern, urban, popular culture.

Death rates have declined, too. Life expectancies, which are a rough indication of quality of life and well-being, have increased dramatically in South Asia. The average Indian born today may reasonably expect to live to the age of 63. When India gained independence in 1947, life expectancy was less than 50 years.

Another measure of well-being is the infant mortality rate. This is perhaps the saddest demographic (population) statistic. It is the number of deaths among children younger than one year of age for every 1,000 children born. In India and Bangladesh, for every 1,000 children born, 66 do not survive to their first birthday. The rate is even higher in Pakistan, where 91 babies for every 1,000 born die in their first year. In comparison, the infant mortality rate in the United States is 6.9 deaths per 1,000. Even with population pressures and poverty, however, most South Asians are much better off today than ever before. There is less famine and starvation, less illness, and less grinding poverty, and the people live much longer and more productive lives.

Population Issues

Population control is difficult. To make matters more difficult, the government is not always trusted on population issues, especially in India. This mistrust may be traced back to the forced sterilization of males in the 1970s, which was a highly unpopular policy. India, too, is a democracy, and coercive policies (those forced onto the people) have led to politicians losing office in the next election.

In addition to the problem of overpopulation is rapid urbanization. People are flocking to cities in search of a better life. They hope to find gainful employment and other opportunities, including better health care and educational programs for their children. Today, about one person in three lives in a city. In a few years, this will increase dramatically. This massive rural-to-urban migration, combined with rapid population growth, will produce gargantuan cities. With 18 million people in the metropolitan area, Mumbai already has more people than New York City. It is projected to become the world's second-largest city in the next 10 years, with more than 26 million inhabitants! It will then be larger than New York City and Chicago combined!

Other huge cities are in the region. By the year 2015, population geographers believe that five of the world's 11 largest cities will be located in South Asia. The smallest of the five will have 17 million people, about as many as the metropolitan area of New York City today! Cities with more than 10 million people are called "megacities." It remains to be seen how these cities will be managed. Then, as now, they will be overcrowded and lack proper sanitation and clean water—yet they are places of hope for tens of millions of rural people in this region.

Another population problem is the sex ratio. This is the number of women for every 100 men, or vice versa. In many developed countries such as the United States and Canada, there are more women than men simply because women live longer. For all of the countries of South Asia, however, women are outnumbered by men. This is because women have lower status and are treated with less care throughout their lives. Poorer care has resulted in higher death rates among females, especially infants. As technologies such as ultrasound devices become more common, the problem will likely get much worse before it gets better. Ultrasound already is illegally used to determine the sex of a fetus. If the fetus is female, it is more likely to be aborted. Male children are believed to be more "valuable," primarily because they can care for their parents when the parents become elderly.

Looming over and complicating the issues of poverty, quality of life, gender equality, and environmental impacts is the sheer magnitude of people in South Asia. These issues are difficult enough in most developing country settings, but in this case their scale is magnified immensely. The continued steady population growth forecast for the next 50 years will only complicate matters further.

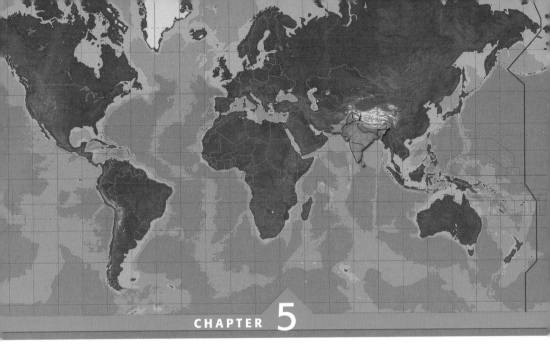

CHAPTER 5

Culture and Society

Although unique among the world's culture regions, South Asia has great diversity in itself. There are dozens of languages, hundreds of dialects, and, in India, slight variations in religious practice from village to village. Whereas Pakistan, Bangladesh, and other small South Asian countries are somewhat homogeneous in terms of culture, India is the epitome of cultural diversity. This diversity is wrapped into the traditions of rural life that have been established over millennia and have led to the development of a number of distinctive social practices, most notably the caste system.

Low caste Hindu villagers (foreground) fetching water from a pond where water buffalos swim, as higher caste Hindus (background) use a separate part of the pond to collect water in Bawrala village, 15.5 miles (25 kilometers) south of Jaipur in India's northwestern Rajasthan state. Although India's 3,000-year-old caste system is supposed to have been abolished (discrimination on the grounds of caste is now illegal), it continues in thousands of villages like this one.

TRADITIONAL RURAL LIFE
Villages and Communities

For most of the past 5,000 years, people of South Asia have lived as rural people and tillers of the soil. In villages scattered across an agricultural landscape, lives have changed little from generation to generation. During this long time span, many traditions evolved and became deeply rooted. To understand South Asia, therefore, one must know the most important traditions that have developed during this 5,000-year history.

The basic social unit in traditional society is the agricultural village. Within this basic social unit, people occupy several roles in a number of social relationships. Playing the largest role is caste. Caste (discussed in detail later in this chapter) is vaguely similar to social class but much more intense and complex. Even today, in rural villages, caste indicates status, determines a person's occupation, and limits with whom he or she can interact. In a tradition-bound society, one can never escape one's caste. For many people, a family name is an indication of caste and occupation. Occupation was almost always governed by caste. For example, a *Dhobi* is a washer man and a *Chamar* a worker in leathercraft. Both are lower-caste activities. Because leatherwork involves dead animals, including cows, it is practiced among the lowest castes.

The second tradition is that most village land is owned by upper-caste elites and is rented out to lower-caste share-croppers (poor tenants). In some cases, these upper-caste landowners are cruel and powerful and exploit the tenants by buying their surplus crops at a very low price and charging high rents. If the tenant falls into debt to the landowner, money lenders or even the landowners loan the tenant money at unbearable interest rates. Such debts carry over from generation to generation. This further serves to exploit poor agricultural laborers.

The ultimate authority used to be the community. With invading empires, including the British, such authority was transferred to the imperial or similar government. The British took full advantage of using the landowners as intermediaries in the extraction of land-based taxes, leading to further injustice on the part of landlords. Land reform since India gained independence has redistributed land ownership so that it is more fair and less exploitative. This land reform has been less successful in some parts of India because local landowners have threatened, attacked, and even killed those who try to break the cycle.

Farming

The benefit of the traditional agricultural system is that it provides food security, meaning that food crops are regularly and reliably produced. Times of plenty are unusual, but with this security, famine is rare. The disadvantage is that this agricultural system is very unproductive. (If it were not for gains in productivity for rice and wheat cultivation that came in the 1960s and 1970s, South Asia would likely not meet its food demands as well as it does today. These gains came with the introduction of new hybrid varieties of wheat and rice.) This lack of productivity occurs largely because of social tradition.

Even today land is not fairly distributed. Many of the landowners are absentee landlords who have more interest in collecting rents than in agricultural production. This is a problem because if someone rents land instead of owning it, he is less likely to make the necessary investments to improve the quality of the land. If the farmers are deep in debt to the landowner, they will not be able to purchase modern chemical fertilizers or farm equipment.

Also, many landholdings are small and scattered; that is, they are fragmented. Small, scattered bits of land are difficult to farm efficiently. The fragmentation is mostly a result of traditional inheritance laws. Under these laws, inherited lands are distributed to each son in a family. Each surviving son gets an equal share of land with good agricultural soils, well-drained land, and so on. This practice means that land is divided into smaller and smaller pieces to accommodate the custom of distributing land evenly.

Many peasant farmers avoid risk. They are afraid to try new methods of farming that might be more productive because they are fearful of failure. They are often so poor that if an investment in a new method of farming does not work out profitably, the loss will push them beyond their normal indebtedness and trap them even deeper in poverty. Farmers normally prefer to grow a reliable food crop for their own consumption rather than a profitable cash crop from which they could earn extra money. They simply cannot afford the chance of failure.

Another major reason for poor agricultural productivity is infrastructural problems. A poor rural road network, a lack of railroad access, and few intermediate companies to buy the farmer's goods limit farmers' ability to get agricultural products to market.

Even with rapid urban growth and migration from the countryside to the cities, more than two-thirds of all Indians today are agricultural-based rural dwellers. Life remains the same as it was generations earlier for tens of millions in South Asia.

Village Governance

Rural life is not solely agricultural: Most people live in or near a village. Social life in a village is tradition-bound, with family, caste, and the *panchayat* (village council) as the most important social elements. Membership on the panchayat was hereditary and based on caste. Typically, there were five members or *panches* (panches means "five"). Since India became independent, efforts to make the panchayat more democratic through elections have been made, but often the power in the hands of the hereditary elite.

CASTE SYSTEM

In no society are all members completely equal. The role and position of citizens within the hierarchy of social status varies from culture to culture. Social geographers refer to how status is ranked as *social stratification.*

South Asia is dominated by the caste system. The caste system is closely tied to the Hindu faith, but it pervades all aspects of society, especially in India and Nepal. This system is assigned by birth and hereditary. It divides people into five broad categories, or *varna*, which means "color." Social interaction is governed by caste: A person is limited to marrying within his or her caste, and social roles, including occupation, are limited and defined by caste. As another example, the priests in charge of a temple can only be Brahmins, the highest caste.

Along with the five broad categories, there are thousands of subcategories of caste called "jati." Some castes are often limited to certain regions. Traditionally, there were even sub-castes for leatherworkers (*Chamar*), those who wash clothes (*Dhobi*), and even haircutters (*Nai*). Other social rules related to ritual are also caste distinct. Adult male Brahmins oftentimes have a looped ropelike or "sacred thread" adornment under their clothes. Even one's last name may indicate caste. Family names such as Mookherjee and Chatterjee are names that only Brahmins have. The -jee (sometimes "-ji") is the clue that indicates a Brahmin family.

The custom of dividing society by caste is perhaps 4,000 years old. It is believed to date from the efforts of the fair-skinned Aryans to distinguish themselves from the darker-skinned people that they had conquered. This is why the term *varna* is used to indicate caste. As the system developed and the Aryans assimilated with the existing population, more categories of caste emerged. How one is assigned caste is a function of *karma*, a reward or punishment through incarnation (rebirth) for actions in a previous life. One is bound by duty, or *dharma*, to follow the rules of caste.

The five broad categories of caste, from the highest status level down, are *Brahmin, Kshatriya, Vaisya, Sudra*, and those people who are considered unworthy of being assigned to a caste. This last group is referred to as the "untouchables," or *Dalits*, and rank at the very bottom. To provide an idea of how status varies, some Brahmins believe that they become polluted if they are touched by or share the same space with a Dalit.

Brahmins form the priestly and teacher caste. Over time, they became the wealthy, landowning caste and today are the most highly educated and urban oriented. The Kshatriyas, or warrior caste, also became a landowning and merchant caste over time. Occupations associated with the Vaisya caste include mercantile (retail trade) jobs and farming. There is a wide gap in status between these first three (Brahmin, Kshatriya, and Vaisya) castes and the next rank, which is the Sudras. The majority of Hindus are Sudras. Occupationally, most are farmers, artisans who weave baskets and produce metalwork, or carpenters.

A full category lower are those who do the most menial of all work and complete the tasks viewed by the others as "unclean." These are individuals without caste. These social outcasts are often referred to as "untouchables" because those of higher status believe that their touch is polluting. Cleaning toilets and sewers, disposing of the dead, and leatherworking (with dead animals, including the sacred cow) are among the occupations most closely associated with this group. As mentioned earlier, these untouchables are today referred to as "Dalits." Often, they are treated with little or no respect. They are not allowed to enter temples, are banned from certain roads, and are even prohibited from wearing sandals in some parts of south India.

The caste system is in many ways rigidly oppressive. It has been used to justify and legitimize prejudice and discrimination. Those of lower caste sometimes are prohibited from touching higher caste individuals or are restricted from sharing food or living quarters. In some places, by tradition, if an individual from the lowest castes came into contact with the shadow of a Brahmin, it meant death! This segregation is much like the racial discrimination in the American South prior to the 1960s. Dalits oftentimes were banned from entering temples for fear that they might pollute the sacred site by their presence. Some Brahmins felt contaminated if they even saw an untouchable. At the same time, caste often involved reciprocal social obligations and economic relations. In theory, at least, there existed some interdependence between castes, so although the system was exploitative and divisive, it was also somewhat functional.

The mass social changes that occur with urbanization, development, and modernization have weakened the caste system. Furthermore, the moral leadership of important leaders, most notably Mahatma Gandhi, has worked to eliminate the most discriminatory practices. Gandhi protested against untouchables not being allowed into temples; however, the bonds of caste remain very strong today, particularly in rural areas. To escape caste, people sometimes change names, discarding a name if it indicates a certain lower caste. Some people convert from Hinduism to other faiths, though often the stigma of caste remains. Still others simply move to a city in an effort to start life anew. The government, too, has made efforts to eliminate caste bias by reserving a certain share of jobs to those of lower or no caste. This reservation system is proving highly controversial to people of all castes. Members of the upper castes, in particular, believe it to be a form of reverse discrimination. Members of lower castes see the system as either not offering enough or full of loopholes.

RELIGION

Diversity of language in South Asia is matched by diversity of religion. Like language, many patterns of faith in South Asia are the product of migrations and invasions. As is the case with Christianity, even under the broad umbrella of one faith, practices and beliefs range widely. The major faiths of South Asia, listed by number of adherents, include Hinduism and Islam, followed by Christianity, Buddhism, Sikhism, Jainism, Zoroastrianism, and animistic faiths. Hinduism and Islam account for about 95 percent of the total. Unlike most areas of the world, many of the smaller regions of South Asia have great religious diversity, with many faiths practiced in close geographic proximity. This has led to local religious conflict. At the same time, however, diversity has played a significant role in forming unique local cultures and in the sharing of religious ideas.

Shown here are the Krishna and Shiva temples, Durbar Square, Bkaktapur, Nepal. Nepal is the world's only Hindu kingdom.

Hinduism

Hinduism is the faith of the overwhelming majority of India and Nepal. Four out of every five Indians is a Hindu, the term for someone who practices Hinduism. Nepal has the distinction of being the world's only Hindu kingdom. Hinduism is also practiced by a substantial minority in Pakistan, Bangladesh, and Sri Lanka.

Hinduism is among the world's oldest faiths, with roots that can be traced back more than 5,000 years. Hinduism represents a fusion between beliefs of the Dravidians, who occupied and dominated parts of India until about 3,500 years ago, and the Aryans, who invaded from central Asia and subdued the Dravidians. As these two groups assimilated, certain of the Dravidians' gods or deities were absorbed into the religious beliefs of the conquering Aryans.

A popular perception is that Hinduism is a polytheistic faith, with belief in many gods, rather than a monotheistic faith, with belief in one god. There are many god figures within Hinduism, but many followers consider these deities little more than manifestations of the one true god, Brahma. Brahma may appear as Vishnu the Creator or as Shiva the Destroyer. Most Hindu temples celebrate, or venerate, either Vishnu or Shiva.

Hindus believe in reincarnation, the idea that humans are reborn. With each rebirth, the merit of one's previous life determines the quality of the new life. If a person demonstrates good karma (living ethically) in one life, the next life will be much better. A person's caste, then, is believed to be determined by the karma exhibited in a previous life. The highest achievement is to escape this cycle of rebirth and be fully absorbed into Brahma. Brahmins are supposedly closest to finishing this cycle.

As Christianity has the Bible as its divine source, Hinduism has several sacred books. These include the ancient *Vedas,* which were put into words about 3,000 years ago. The Vedas contain the philosophical foundations of Hinduism and are the source of great epic stories. Natural landmarks play a prominent role in these tales. The Ganges River is referred to as a sacred body, and today it is treated as sacred. By bathing in the Ganges, a person may cleanse his or her soul. The river is considered the sacred and proper resting place for one's spirit, and so many people are cremated and have their ashes cast into it. Many pilgrimage sites throughout India draw their attraction from their appearance in the Vedas, just as Jerusalem is the destination of pilgrimages by Christians, Muslims, and Jews.

Because of historical isolation and blending of faiths, Hinduism varies remarkably from place to place, with some gods being extremely important in one village and not very important in the next. Practices also vary from place to place. Hinduism is not a proselytizing faith, meaning that believers do not attempt to convert others. Rather, it is an ethnic religion into which one must be born.

Islam

Islam is the most important faith in Pakistan (95 percent of the population) and Bangladesh (83 percent) and the second most prevalent faith in India (14 percent). Pakistan is officially an Islamic republic, and politics there are dominated by religious institutions. Among these are the *madrassas*, or religious schools. Those who adhere to Islam are called "Muslims."

Islam was founded in Saudi Arabia in the year 622 by the Prophet Muhammad. Its founding was followed by rapid spread westward across most of North Africa and eastward toward South Asia. In less than a century, Islam had reached what is now Pakistan. Invasions by Islamic peoples from Persia and Central Asia eventually led to the establishment of a series of kingdoms in South Asia that culminated with rule by the Muslim Moguls. As was noted in Chapter 3, the Moguls ruled with an iron fist and sought to spread their faith widely. Conversion was often coerced, but Islam did appeal to many Hindus. First, Muslims believe in the equality of man. To a Hindu of low caste, or those without caste status, this can be very appealing. Wherever rule by Muslim kings and emperors occurred for extended periods of time, conversions to Islam were significant in number.

There are many contrasts between Hinduism and Islam. One example can be found in diet. Hindus believe that cows are sacred and so do not consume beef. Muslims, on the other hand, are repulsed by pork, which they view as unclean. With so many followers of each faith living side by side, conflict often occurs. Occasionally, these differences result in protests and riots that become violent. Colonial rulers recognized the opportunity to pit one group against the others, as do many politi-

Pakistani Muslims attend Friday prayers outside the Red Mosque in Islamabad, Pakistan. Islam was founded in the year 622 by the Prophet Muhammad. It is the most important faith in Pakistan.

cians today who take advantage of cultural differences in order to gain political advantage. Controversially, too, many Muslim mosques occupy sites venerated, or worshiped, by Hindus.

Buddhism

Buddhism does not have many followers in South Asia, although it is the leading faith in Sri Lanka. Still, its historical impact on the region is immense. Buddhism was founded by a Hindu prince in about 500 B.C. in what is now north central India. This prince, Siddhartha, came to realize his goal while sitting underneath a Bodhi tree. That place is now the city of Bodhgaya, a pilgrimage site for many Buddhists.

Buddhism spread from India to China, Japan, and Southeast Asia, where it remains a leading faith. It became immediately popular in South Asia because it offered a contrast to the rigid rules of the caste system. When the great emperor Asoka converted to Buddhism, he spread the appealing message of optimism and castelessness far and wide. Gradually, Hinduism moderated somewhat and absorbed aspects of Buddhism. Buddha eventually came to be viewed as an aspect, or incarnation, of Brahma.

Jainism

Jainism, too, originated as a protest movement of sorts against the oppressive aspects of Hinduism. Today, there are perhaps 3 million Jains, who live mostly in western India. Jains share many beliefs with Hindus, including reincarnation and eventual salvation. The faith also is nonproselytizing, and Jains revere life and are strict vegetarians. Some Jains are so strict in this belief that they wear cloth over their mouths to avoid accidentally swallowing insects. Because of their vegetarianism, they often became merchants and have emerged as a wealthy and influential group, especially in Mumbai.

Zoroastrianism

Zoroastrianism is nearly as old as Hinduism, dating back to the seventh century B.C. This once wide-ranging faith numbers only about 100,000 followers. It is does not seek new members, and followers of the faith must marry within the religion. As with

Jains, they have become successful businesspeople, wielding much power and influence even with their small numbers.

Christianity

Christians form substantial minorities in several parts of India, especially in the southern state of Kerala. They are a majority in two of the far northeastern hill states. Like converts to other religions, most converts to this proselytizing faith are lower-caste Hindus who are perhaps dissatisfied with the rigid and oppressive social code of Hinduism.

Sikhism

As a blend of the elements of Hinduism and Islam, Sikhism is an important regional faith. Centered on the Indian state of Punjab, the faith first offered a fresh spirituality that released Hindus from the confines of caste with appealing aspects of Islam. Sikh men may be easily identified on the street by five distinctive ornaments, or *kakkars*. These are most noticeably the *kesh,* a turban that hides their uncut hair, and the *kirpan*, or sword, which often is decorative but sometimes real. Less obvious are the other three kakkars: the *kanga*, a wooden or ivory comb; *kacha*, or special shorts; and *kara*, a steel bracelet. In part because of an optimistic attitude, Sikhs have become known for being successful and productive farmers and great engineers. Sikhs have long agitated for an independent state to be called Khalistan. In retribution for the government's forceful takeover of the Golden Temple (the faith's holiest site), Indira Gandhi's Sikh bodyguards assassinated her in 1984. Tensions remain high in the area of Punjab even today.

Animism

There are a number of animistic faiths in India. These are prevalent in the hilly remote areas, especially parts of the northeast states and the east central region. These belief systems are the remnants of the pre-Dravidian peoples and only remain in areas largely inaccessible to invaders, missionaries, and migrants.

Temples and Pilgrimages

South Asia has breathtaking religious landscapes. Thousands of religious temples and shrines have been constructed in the past five millennia. Many of these serve as pilgrimage sites today, just as the Vatican does for Catholics from all over the world.

LANGUAGE

The diversity of language in South Asia is mind-boggling. India alone has 15 official languages. More than 1,000 distinct languages and 22,000 dialects have been identified. The pattern of this diversity reflects the history of migrations across the region. Of the five major language groups, the Indo-Aryan and Dravidian languages claim nearly 98 percent of the population as speakers. These two language groups have little in common with one another. In fact, English shares common roots with Hindi (an Indo-Aryan language) and resembles it more so than any Dravidian language.

Language can be a controversial topic in South Asia. English use is widespread among the most educated, but there is some resentment against its speakers because it was a language imposed on a colonized people. In a similar manner, many people in south India resent the use of Hindi, a language of north India. They feel that Hindi is being forced on them. Other languages are particular to specific ethnic groups, and for many of the people, their language is their identity. In some cases, language unites them in a push to break away from India. There are also the practicalities of having 15 official languages: In what languages should government documents be printed? What should be the language for education? Should political boundaries be drawn on the basis of language use? Each of these questions has generated controversy since India gained independence in 1947 and likely will do so for the next half-century.

Bangladesh school children hold a poster that reads "Buy a Book, Read a Book, and Write a Book," in Dhaka, February 1, 2002, to observe the 1952 Bengali Language Movement, considered the sparking point that eventually led to an independent Bangladesh.

The most prominent Indo-Aryan languages are Hindi and Urdu, the tongues that dominate northern India and Pakistan, respectively. Hindi is closer to the original Sanskrit introduced by the Aryans. It is the most common language for television, newspapers, magazines, and movies and has 300 million speakers. It is the most universally used language in India and is most commonly the first language in a broad band across northern India that is sometimes referred to as the "Hindi Belt." Urdu is similar but incorporates Persian and Arabic words and was brought in by Muslim invaders. In areas where Islam became more prevalent, Urdu also became more prevalent. Bengali is also a leading language with more than 240 million speakers. It is a distinctive Indo-Aryan language spoken in Bangladesh and in the state of West Bengal in India. There are a number of regional languages, some more and others less closely resembling Hindi. Millions of people speak these languages, as well.

The leading Dravidian languages are all spoken in southern India or Sri Lanka. Each roughly corresponds to a given state's boundaries. These are Tamil, in the state of Tamil Nadu; Kannada, in Karnataka; Telugu, in Andhra Pradesh; Malayalam, in Kerala; and Sinhalese, in the country of Sri Lanka.

English is still an important language as a result of the colonial dominance of the courts, administration, and learning for more than 200 years. It is a language of instruction in many universities and, along with Hindi, serves as a *lingua franca*, or common trade language, for business and governmental elites.

FOOD AND DIET

Indian food brings a kaleidoscope of sensations! Traditional cuisine in South Asia varies with the ecology of an area and its cultural practices. In areas where rice is dominant, this staple grain provides the basis for meals. Where wheat is commonly grown, a wide variety of very tasty breads is available. With so many Muslims who abhor pork, and Hindus who will not consume beef, many areas are nearly or entirely vegetarian. The south especially is vegetarian. Chicken is the only meat consumed throughout India, although lamb and seafood are popular in certan areas.

Preparation of meals may involve slow cooking and use of two dozen or more different spices. Curry is not a particular spice; it is actually a mix of whatever spices a particular cook uses. A *masala* is a mix of spices in a certain combination. The word even means "mix." The use of various peppers sometimes makes the food spicy hot. For poorer people, the variety of food is very limited. A simple and very common meal is rice with *dhal* (cooked beans or other lentils). Tea or "chai" is a popular drink. It is usually served with much milk and sugar. Food is eaten with fingers, typically those of the right hand. As a complement to a meal, one may chew *pan,* a collection of spices and other condiments that usually includes betel nut.

FAMILY LIFE

With so many cultural influences, some aspects of family life are distinct from region to region across South Asia. Those discussed here related mostly to major transitions in people's lives—birth, marriage, and death.

Marriages today are usually arranged. Parents try to marry their children to people of the same caste (if they are Hindu) or faith. "Love marriages," where the bride and groom choose one another, are becoming more common, particularly in cities, but they are still the exception. Dowry is often associated with marriage. A dowry is a gift given to the groom's family by the family of the bride. It is controversial, because it implies a lower value for women and even equates women to the amount of dowry they bring. "Dowry deaths," the killing of brides in such a way that appears to be an accident, are rare, but they do occur. Estimates range as high as 15,000 annually. A typical "accident" involves "mistakenly" spilling kerosene onto the bride's clothes and having them catch fire. This happens most often in cases where the groom's family felt that the dowry was too little or insulting.

The British banned the practice of *sutee*, when a widow climbed onto her husband's funeral pyre, but it continues today, particularly in more remote areas. Traditionally, women have lower status and often are treated as possessions of their husband. Even today, widows have a low socioeconomic status. To be a Dalit widow is the lowest social station in life.

With knowledge of the practices discussed in this chapter, one can better understand and appreciate the complexity of South Asia's cultures. Oftentimes travelers, whether businesspeople or tourists, Americans or others, gain only a hint of the region's tremendous diversity of cultures. A better understanding of these cultural patterns allows for a deeper appreciation of and better connections with the region's peoples.

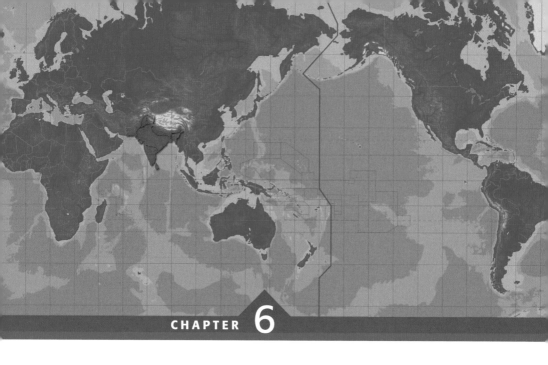

CHAPTER 6

Political History

A variety of factors places South Asia at the center of world affairs. Many of these factors result from the region's political history. Animosities between Pakistan and India, always a concern, are especially sensitive now that each possesses atomic weapons. Afghanistan and parts of Pakistan serve as refuges for terrorists, including al Qaeda. Finally, the region's huge population makes it an important player on the world stage.

MODERN SOUTH ASIA

At midnight on August 15, 1947, the modern history of South Asia began. After nearly a century of colonial rule over the subcontinent, the British, simply "quit India." They left in a rush, less than six months after stating their intention to finally withdraw. Little attention was given to how the newly independent area would be governed. Pushed by popular leaders such as Mohandas K. Gandhi, the British colonial government simply walked away from its most prized colonial possession, what had been the "jewel in the crown" of the British Empire.

Long awaited by the peoples of South Asia, this moment was accompanied by tragedy rarely matched in human history. This tragedy, known as the Partition of India, involved perhaps the greatest forced migration of people the world has ever known. What events led to independence? What did it mean for the British to "quit India"? What was the great tragedy and why or how did it occur?

The Road to Independence

Leaders of British India had long agitated for independence. A core group of well-educated, elite leaders had pushed for increased self-governance and eventual independence. The greatest leader, however, was the one who discarded his elite appearance and advocated for the masses of South Asians who were poor. This was Mohandas K. Gandhi. Instead of wearing the garb of Europeans or wealthy Indians, he was nearly always dressed in a *dhoti*, a simple garment that resembles a loincloth. This is the garment worn by the poorest of Indians.

His philosophy, although rooted in Hinduism, was respectful of those of all faiths and all backgrounds. He also believed in nonviolence, including open protest. This doctrine of nonviolence, or *ahimsa,* was later adopted by civil rights leaders in the United States, including Dr. Martin Luther King, Jr. So revered and respected did Gandhi become that he was referred to as *Mahatma*, which means "Great Soul."

Gandhi, whose life was profiled in an Academy-Award-winning movie, demonstrated persistence and right moral action throughout the push for independence. His goal was to demonstrate that British colonial rule was neither moral nor

Mohandas "Mahatma" Gandhi, right, laughs with the man who was the nation's first prime minister, Jawaharlal Nehru, left, at the All-India Congress committee meeting in Bombay, India, on July 6, 1946. Gandhi's philosophy of nonviolent resistance, including civil disobedience and fasts, drove India to independence in 1947 after nearly 200 years of British rule. Gandhi was assassinated in 1948 for his tolerance of other religions.

right. Gandhi used several strategies—prolonged hunger strikes, long marches, and impassioned and articulate speeches and interviews—to stress his point. Through his actions, he became a moral force and role model rarely matched in the twentieth century. His most famous protest was his march to the sea to make salt. The British had imposed an unfair salt tax and banned the production and sale of salt, something necessary to all. To protest, Gandhi walked 240 miles to the sea and gathered a small amount of salt. By doing this, Gandhi, already more than 60 years old, broke the law. He then urged his fellow countrymen to follow his lead, which generated mass protest.

Not only did Gandhi help liberate India and the other nations of South Asia, he also broke down social barriers. His efforts also gave greater social respect to the Dalits, whom he called *Harijans*, or "children of God." Before Gandhi's protests, many Dalits were not allowed to enter Hindu temples, even though they were Hindu!

Other key events helped destroy the myth of the British as enlightened rulers and push them from the region. In 1919, General Dyer, a colonial military official, declared a ban on all public gatherings in the city of Amritsar and the surrounding region. A crowd formed to protest this suspension of free speech. Dyer ordered troops to open fire into the crowd without warning. Trapped in a confined space and fired on at point-blank range, hundreds of unarmed men, women, and children were killed or seriously injured in the panic. The outrage over this tragedy brought Indians closer together and gave renewed strength, determination, and unity to their fight for independence. The British, who often sought to justify their rule as enlightened, could no longer make this claim in light of the butchery that had occurred.

"QUIT INDIA" AND PARTITION

Why did the British finally "quit India" in such a rapid and sloppy manner? They had recognized for many years that India's independence was inevitable. The withdrawal in the late 1940s came about for two reasons. World War II had just ended, and the British, who had just escaped defeat by Hitler's Nazi Germany, could not rightly say that colonial rule was morally superior. Also, the British people were tired of war and wanted to focus on rebuilding their own war-weary country. The British public was not interested in maintaining a large, overextended empire over peoples that should have had the power to govern themselves.

The viceroy of India, Lord Mountbatten, a prominent member of the British Royal Family, immediately made efforts to have the colonial rulers to withdraw, setting the date of August 15, 1947. Unfortunately, the sudden and hasty withdrawal led to a very poor geographical arrangement in terms of what the map of South Asia would look like. South Asia, commonly referred to as "British India" during the colonial period, was quite messy in a political sense. Key differences in language, ethnicity, religion, and administration existed. Each of these differences worked toward splintering the newly independent land into perhaps dozens, if not hundreds, of smaller countries. The potential for conflict was tremendous. It is truly amazing that, ultimately, only six countries comprised South Asia— rather than nearly 600.

POLITICAL DIVISION OF SOUTH ASIA

Administratively and culturally, two broad divisions existed within the British colony. First, there were the areas directly controlled by the British. Second, there were hundreds of large, medium-sized, and small kingdoms that relied on the colonial rulers for legitimacy. These princely states, numbering an incredible 596, were a product of the "divide and rule" strategy. They were allowed to exist because the British used them to more easily exploit differences between local and regional interests, whether based on caste, religion, language, or ethnicity. The British would play one group against the other by allocating power differently or by assigning benefits to one group at the expense of another. The princely states were a convenient way for the British to have broad control without the enormous costs of direct control. Some of these princes were Muslim, others Hindu. In some cases, Hindus ruled over Muslims or vice versa.

Religious differences led to pressures to create several countries, with some extreme groups demanding independent states

Muslim refugees cram into coaches and the roof of a train bound for Pakistan from a New Delhi area, India, on September 26, 1947, after India's independence and partition on August 15.

for Muslim, Hindu, Buddhist, or Sikh peoples. Language and other cultural differences also led to people wanting countries, or at least states within countries, that were based on language or ethnicity. The strongest tension was between Muslims and Hindus. Riots and protests led to bloodshed, as extremists from each group targeted the other. Some Hindu nationalists were upset with Gandhi's message of accommodation and peace. In January 1948, one such extremist shot and killed the Mahatma, sparking yet another round of retribution.

Those who wanted South Asia to be one country were to be disappointed. Escalating violence meant that it would be best to split most of South Asia into two countries—India, which would be largely be Hindu, and Pakistan, which would be predominantly Muslim. The drawing of the boundaries could only be a sad compromise, as many Hindus lived in majority Muslim areas and many Muslims lived among a Hindu or even Sikh majority. To make matters worse, Muslim Pakistan would have two parts, East Pakistan (which is now Bangladesh) and West Pakistan (today's Pakistan), separated by 900 miles (1,450 kilometers).

The political division into Hindu India and Muslim Pakistan forced millions of people to leave lands on which they had lived for generations. Many were forced to leave property and possessions and move great distances, and those who migrated endured robbery, looting, rape, and murder. The bitter feelings, lost livelihoods, and economic costs spurred even more bloodletting. In total, about 15 million people were relocated in the short time span after Partition, and the journeys claimed an estimated 250,000 lives.

MODERN COUNTRIES

Seven countries now compose South Asia. Five of those—India, Pakistan, Sri Lanka, Nepal, and Bhutan—could be counted immediately after the British withdrawal. Bangladesh, formerly East Pakistan, split from Pakistan in 1971. India is now a secular state, or country not governed by religious leaders, even though the majority of its people are Hindu. Pakistan is officially an Islamic state, and Bangladesh has a Muslim majority. Sri Lanka is primarily Buddhist and has a large minority of Hindus. Nepal is the world's only Hindu kingdom, and tiny Bhutan is an isolated and remote Buddhist kingdom. Each state has its own story to tell of the postcolonial period.

India

Since becoming independent, India has remained relatively stable and democratic. It is the world's largest democracy in terms of population and should serve as a role model to newly democratic countries. Early leaders recognized the value of a stable, strong, secular central government. They made every effort to protect these goals during the country's early years of independence. Because of their success, India is the most politically stable and democratic nation in South Asia. Even in this democratic system, however, one family has dominated the country's politics for four decades. The longest-serving and most powerful leaders of India have been members Gandhi family (not related to Mahatma Gandhi). India's first prime minister was Jawaharlal Nehru. His daughter, Indira Gandhi, became prime minister several years after his death. She was followed shortly by her son, Rajiv. Now, their political party (the Indian National Congress Party) is led by Sonia Gandhi, Rajiv's widow. Much like the Kennedy family in the United States, the Gandhi family has been characterized by great tragedy and sorrow. Each of these leaders deserves attention.

Nehru

Before India became independent, Jawaharlal Nehru was among Mahatma Gandhi's most trusted senior advisors. Educated at the best British schools and from an elite family, he led India with a steady and principled hand. He made every effort to keep India a secular state and made sure that it had a strong central government. Although against British rule, he did respect and work to keep some British institutions, such as an able civil service and a strong university system. He also had a respect for science and believed that scientific study would help solve many problems of the day. Nehru believed that careful planning and investment was a way to plant the seeds of future prosperity. Under his leadership, the country followed long-term planning programs and made great investments in heavy industries. He was never oppressive and was much respected as

Indira Gandhi, Prime Minister of India, is shown in a 1967 photo. She was elected in 1966, voted out of office in 1977, then re-elected in 1980.

a stable leader for the new country. His death in 1962 left the nation mourning the loss of one of its founding fathers.

Indira Gandhi

Largely because of her father's reputation, Indira Gandhi was elected prime minister in 1966. Those who backed her calculated that because she was young and female, she would be easily controlled. They were very disappointed when she proved to be a strong and independent politician. She became increasingly dictatorial, however, and relied heavily on her eldest son, Sanjay, to direct government affairs. Perhaps her most controversial decision was a population planning program in which tens of thousands of males were forcibly sterilized. When threatened politically, she declared martial law. Her declaration was very unpopular, and when martial law was lifted and elections were held in 1977, she was booted out of office. The newly elected leaders, however, were poorly organized. The prime minister elected to succeed her became known not for his policies but for his practice of drinking a glass of urine daily! In 1980, less than three years after being voted out of office, Indira Gandhi was voted back in. In 1984, she authorized the military to storm the Golden Temple, the holiest site in Sikhdom, to root out militants. "Operation Bluestar" outraged many Sikhs. Soon thereafter, in retribution, she was assassinated by two members of her own bodyguard, both of whom were Sikhs. More than 30 bullets made sure that the task was complete. Her murder sparked revenge riots across the country, leaving thousands dead.

Rajiv Gandhi

Before 1980, Rajiv Gandhi had no interest in politics and was content to be an airline pilot. His mother convinced him to enter politics after his brother Sanjay's death in a plane crash. Boosted by the popularity of his mother and grandfather, he became India's prime minister in 1985. Despite a bribery scandal, his administration was seen as open-minded and a breath of fresh air. He introduced financial reforms that helped stimulate the economy. In trying to stabilize politics in neighboring Sri Lanka, he sent troops to police part of that country and help pacify ethnic Hindu separatists. This proved to be very unpopular among separatists and their sympathizers, and in 1991, while campaigning in southern India, a Sri Lankan Tamil separatist strapped with bombs blew herself up just steps away from Gandhi, killing him and many others.

Sonia Gandhi

After Rajiv's death there was an interlude in the Gandhi family's involvement in politics. His widow, Sonia, and her children withdrew from politics almost entirely. They were disgusted by and fearful of the process that had taken such a toll on their family. During most of the 1990s, a nationalist Hindu party controlled the political scene. Eventually, members of the Congress Party (of which the Gandhi family had been members) convinced Sonia to lead the party. In spring 2004, Sonia Gandhi (who is Italian born) led her Congress Party to victory in national elections but refused to become prime minister.

Pakistan

Much of Pakistan's political history has been characterized by dictatorship and instability. Even today, President Pervez Musharraf is constantly under threat of assassination by an assortment of Muslim militants, criminals, corrupt politicians, and perhaps people in his own military. He survived two close calls in 2004 alone, as bomb blasts nearly struck his motorcades. Musharraf is a military officer who seized power in a peaceful *coup d'etat* (military takeover) in 1999. The country has a history of elected governments alternating with military dictators. Weak and sometimes corrupt elected governments are toppled by military leaders who seek order or power or both.

Bangladesh

Bangladesh (East Pakistan) gained independence in 1971 after a civil war with West Pakistan. West Pakistan held the majority of the country's wealth but a minority of its population. East Pakistan, on the other hand, had most of the people and was a land of grinding poverty. The center of government also was in West Pakistan. East Pakistan, for understandable reasons, resented West Pakistan's wealth; it also resented military and administrative control wielded by leaders located nearly 1,000 miles (1,600 kilometers) away. Momentum for independence built up and exploded into full civil war in 1970. Partly because of the large distance separating the two parts of Pakistan, it was difficult for West Pakistan to keep control over the East.

Like Pakistan, Bangladesh has suffered from political instability. A cycle of elections, takeovers, and new elections characterized the country's politics from 1971 to the late 1980s. Popularly elected and sometimes corrupt leaders have been overthrown by military leaders. Fortunately, since 1991, the elected governments have been stable. Peaceful governance hopefully has taken root in Bangladesh.

Sri Lanka

Sri Lanka (then Ceylon) became an independent country in 1948. Even though it was very close to British India in both distance and culture, Sri Lanka had been administrated separately by the British. On gaining independence, it became the most stable and prosperous nation in South Asia.

Ethnic tensions began to rise between two groups, however; there were the Sinhalese-speaking Buddhists, who are a majority of the population, and the Tamil-speaking Hindus, who are a large minority. Tamils were worried about political domination by Sinhalese. Sinhalese were worried about the threats from Tamil rebels, who were trying to form an independent country in northern Sri Lanka. The political peace finally broke into open fighting between the Tamil "Tigers" and government forces in 1977. This conflict continues today. Periodically, a truce or cease-fire is called, but lasting peace seems to evade the country. India's Prime Minister Rajiv Gandhi tried to stabilize the country by sending peacekeeping forces in the 1980s. Some Tamils perceived this as a threat to their fight for independence. In response, Gandhi was assassinated by a Tamil terrorist. Since 2000, hope for peace has blossomed as leaders on both sides seem to be seeking compromise and are now at least negotiating.

Nepal

Nepal is the world's only Hindu kingdom. Even with a diverse population, it has remained fairly unified since the mid-1700s.

The Nepalese royal family is seen in this picture taken during the coming of age ceremony of Crown Prince Dipendra (left) in 1990. All the family members seen in the photograph are believed to have been killed by the Crown prince, who shot his family and then himself. From left to right: Crown Prince Dipendra, King Birendra, Prince Nirajan, Queen Aiswarya, and Princess Shuriti.

It has been ruled by the same family almost continuously since that time. Since the British withdrew from the region in 1947, there have been periodic calls for greater democracy. As a result, the royal family has given some power to the elected government. Still, the king is relatively powerful. The only consistent challenge to Nepal's stability has been from Communist rebel groups who call themselves Maoists. They have attempted to destabilize the country with armed attacks on settlements. Their threat to the government continues to grow.

In July 2001, a bizarre and brutal incident nearly destroyed the royal family. Crown Prince Dipendra, heir to the throne, was upset at not being allowed to marry the woman of his choice. Always known as a person of violent mood swings, the prince went into a rage and shot his father (the king), mother (the queen), brother, sister, and several other relatives and then committed suicide. The most logical person to take over as king was the dead king's brother, Gyanendra. He quickly established order after this strange event. It had been the world's greatest massacre of a royal family since the entire Russian royal family was executed in 1917.

Bhutan

The smallest nation in South Asia is also the most isolated. The very rugged mountains, along with a king who wants little change, help maintain that isolation. It is not even known how many people live in this remote Buddhist kingdom, although the number is believed to be between 800,000 and 2 million.

Bhutan and the Bhutanese people share more in common culturally with Tibet (in China) than with the rest of South Asia. Most Bhutanese are Buddhists who speak Tibetan languages. About a quarter are Hindus who speak either Hindi or Nepali. Most people (95 percent) are farmers, making their living from the land. The average person is poor and has little formal education.

The current king, named Jigme Singye Wangchuk, consults an elected assembly before he makes major decisions. Change comes slowly in this mountain country as it seeks to protect its culture from outside influences. Only recently has Bhutan begun to develop tourism and its great hydroelectric potential.

Maldives

Four hundred miles off the southwest coast of India are the Maldives, a group of islands that became independent from Britain in 1965. The population of only 310,000 is scattered across 26 island groups. There are an incredible 1,190 islands, the largest of which has an area of only 5 square miles (13 square kilometers). Fishing and tourism are the most important activities.

Politically, the nation was a Muslim kingdom before the British established overall authority in 1887. It has had regular elections, but a significant and sometimes questionable advantage has always been had by the ruling political party.

The country has a number of environmental challenges. Rising sea levels caused by global warming will progressively threaten most of the islands. Rare and unique habitats are being destroyed from these rising sea levels, as well.

GOVERNANCE AND ADMINISTRATION

During the colonial period, most of South Asia was governed under the British model. One might expect, as a result, that many similarities would exist in the way these countries are governed today. In the chaos that followed independence, however, each country developed its own approach to government.

India

India is the world's largest democracy. It takes pride in having a strong record of free and fair elections at both the national and local levels since becoming independent. It also is a federal republic, a country in which the central government is the ultimate authority and governance is by representatives selected by the people, not directly by the people. India is also a parliamentary democracy in which the country's leaders are chosen from the body of elected representatives. In this case, the prime minister is elected from political parties that control the national legislature. The national legislature is called the Lok Sabha and resembles the Canadian or British House of Commons. There is also a president, but this post is limited in power and largely ceremonial. The prime minister is the most powerful politician. India prides itself in having a secular government in which people of all faiths are treated equally and fairly, even though the country is overwhelmingly Hindu.

Pakistan's President, General Pervez Musharraf, answers questions during a press conference in Islamabad, Pakistan, October 8, 2001.

India consists of 29 states and five union territories. The states range greatly in size and population. They govern themselves much like those of the United States. The union territories are more directly controlled by the federal government because of their small size and other special characteristics.

Pakistan

Pakistan is officially an Islamic republic. This means the government is based on representative rule and endorses Islam as the national religion. In practice, however, governance often has been through military decree. President Pervez Musharraf took power in 1999 and announced his intention to stamp out corruption, reestablish civil order, and restore free and fair elections. His task is now complicated by the War on Terror. His alliance with the United States to seek out and destroy terrorism is unpopular in his own country. It remains to be seen whether he can accomplish his objectives.

Pakistan is broken down into five large provinces, each of which has smaller subdivisions. Supposedly, each province is administered from a central provincial government; however, in the Northwest Frontier Province it is said that local tribes hold the power and that not even Pakistani military forces control the area. A stronghold of tribal control and Muslim fundamentalism, this is supposedly an area where Osama bin Laden and other al Qaeda leaders have sought refuge.

Bangladesh

Bangladesh (which means "country of the Bengalis") also is a federal democratic republic. Again, this means that representatives of the people are democratically elected and the central government is the ultimate authority. As noted previously, Bangladesh's government has achieved stability only since 1991. Bangladesh is composed of 22 districts. Each district is further broken down into *tahsils*. There are 481 tahsils; they are equivalent to a county in the United States.

Sri Lanka

Sri Lanka, too, is a federal democratic republic. Control over its territory is limited, however. Tamil rebels control much of the northern part of the island and have made efforts to establish their own order. In 2005, the destructive and bloody civil conflict rages on, although recent negotiations have brought some hope for peace.

Nepal, Bhutan, and the Maldives

Nepal is a hereditary constitutional monarchy ruled by a Hindu king, and Bhutan is a Buddhist kingdom. Nepal's elected assembly does hold some limited power; Bhutan's hold very little. The Maldives is a developing democracy with an elected government.

TRANSPORTATION

Of all the modes of transport that help stitch trade and people together in South Asia, railroads are the most important. The Indian railways are administered by a single governmental entity. With more than 2 million workers, it is has the largest workforce of any nonmilitary employer in the world!

Railroads were first established in the region by the British. They needed to ship raw materials such as cotton to Great Britain to be processed; thus, railroads were needed to link agricultural areas to seaports. Because railroads were a relatively new technology in the mid-1800s, many of them were built with different distances between tracks. The distance between the tracks, called the gauge, is often narrow in mountain areas and wider in other areas. In comparison, railroad tracks in the United States are nearly all "standard gauge": 4 feet 11 inches (1.5 meters) apart.

COMMUNICATIONS

Quality of communications varies widely. Some areas are inaccessible, with little, if any, telephone, Internet, or other connections. At the same time, some areas are as well connected as any in the world. Cell phones are found almost everywhere.

Large software companies are now investing in India. Because they need quality communications, many of them are spending large sums of money for globally connected high-technology research facilities. These high-tech campuses help exploit the potential of highly educated and inexpensive labor in South Asia.

South Asia's political history from the arrival of the Aryans to the colonization by the British has been highly influenced by peoples from outside the region. Over land, as with the Aryans and most others, or by sea, as with the British, these influences have shaped patterns of religion, language, and politics. The economy, too, has been shaped by these influences: The region's potential emergence as an economic powerhouse and the controversies surrounding outsourcing are related to the large number of highly skilled English-speaking college graduates. The fact that English is such a predominant non-native language can be attributed to the British imposing its use as a language of administration.

CHAPTER 7

Economy

Today, most people on the Indian subcontinent are rural and make their living as either agricultural laborers or small, independent farmers. Nonetheless, industrial growth has been rapid. Because all of this realm was once under British colonial rule and because India is the largest component of the realm, this discussion of economy focuses primarily on that country.

AGRICULTURAL LIVELIHOODS

Making a living with agriculture means being sensitive to average environmental conditions and limitations. In a poor agricultural society where there is little room for error, survival depends on knowledge of what the environment will allow. South Asia, for example,

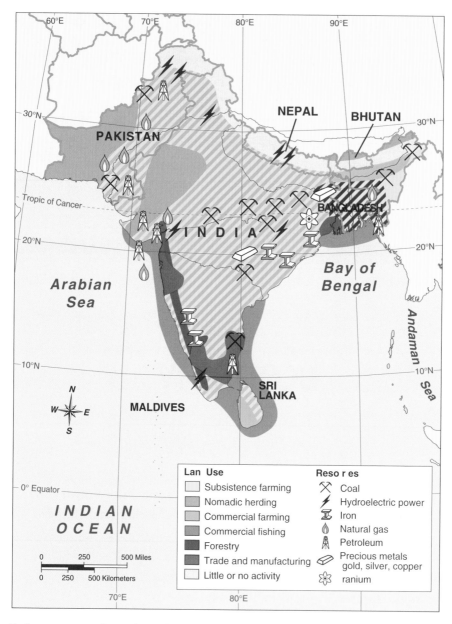

Lan Use		Reso r es	
☐	Subsistence farming	⚒	Coal
▨	Nomadic herding	⚡	Hydroelectric power
☐	Commercial farming	⚒	Iron
▨	Commercial fishing	◊	Natural gas
▨	Forestry	⚚	Petroleum
▨	Trade and manufacturing	▱	Precious metals gold, silver, copper
☐	Little or no activity	☢	ranium

Today, most people on the Indian subcontinent make their living as either agricultural laborers or small, independent farmers. Nonetheless, industrial growth has been rapid. One highly controversial economic area in which India is involved is the outsourcing of call centers and other office activities. Beginning in the late 1990s, and more noticeably after 2000, many global companies relocated service call center activities from the United States to locations in Indian cities such as Mumbai, Bangalore, and Hyderabad.

is dependent on the monsoon climate. Unlike midlatitude climates with four distinct seasons, the monsoon climate of South Asia offers three seasons. There is a hot and wet season, a cooler, drier season, and a hot and dry (yet humid) season. Under these conditions, two major types of traditional food crops can be grown: *kharif,* or wet-season crops, and *rabi,* or dry-season crops.

The monsoons sometimes bring destructive floods, but they always bring the needed rain for crops. Across all of South Asia, however, there is substantial variation in the regularity and quantity of available rainfall. Some parts of South Asia are wetter and therefore more suitable to rice cultivation. Other areas are drier and more suitable to the growing of wheat. Still other regions, such as northwestern India and much of Pakistan, are parched desert where crops can be raised only with use of irrigation. In addition to the kharif and rabi crop seasonal rotation, there are some regional crop specialties.

Rice is the leading staple crop, and the nutritious grain supplies about 40 percent of the region's food needs. It is the dominant crop where fertile river-valley soils, level land, a warm growing season, and plentiful rain are found. Rice is most prevalent in the eastern half of the region. Wheat is the second most important crop and supplies a quarter of the region's food supply. Wheat does not need the plentiful moisture or the warm temperature that rice does. It is grown across the northwest parts of South Asia. There are other crops, called pulses and millets, that are also important in certain regions. Often, rice or wheat is grown in one season, with a second crop grown in the other season.

Agriculture in South Asia changed little in the hundreds of years up to the British colonial period. Since then, change has come very rapidly. The first change came with the growing of cash crops. Early global trade spurred the production of cash crops, or crops that could be sold for cash. Instead of growing food crops for one's own consumption (subsistence farming), a farmer could grow a crop like cotton for sale. Cash earned in the sale could be

An Indian farmer works in a field at the Pakistan-India border, south of Jammu, India. Most people in South Asia make their living as either agricultural laborers or small, independent farmers.

used to purchase food or whatever else the farmer desired. Cotton remains an important cash crop today. Jute, a high-fiber plant used for making rope, also has been historically important as a cash crop. Other cash crops that can sometimes be consumed locally include peanuts, sugar cane, oil seeds, and tea. Some areas in the region are better suited than others for each of these crops.

A second large-scale change in the region's agriculture has been the introduction of irrigation. Today, irrigation that either uses large-scale canal projects or draws on local wells helps water much of South Asia's cultivated land. Crop yields have increased dramatically since the introduction of irrigation. Irrigation projects were started in the 1800s under colonial direction and have expanded dramatically since the end of the colonial period. Irrigation does have some disadvantages. Depending on local circumstances, it can lead to loss of groundwater, water-logged soils, or soils with too many toxic salts left behind as irrigation water evaporates. Some areas are no longer agriculturally productive as a result of these problems.

In South Asia, the "Green Revolution" has produced a tremendous jump in agricultural production. This is especially true for basic foodstuffs such as rice and wheat. Green Revolution is the name given to a combination of several agricultural innovations. It involves use of high-yield varieties of seeds, appropriate use of irrigation water, application of commercial fertilizers, and use of modern technologies, such as tractors for tilling. The Green Revolution has allowed world food production to grow much faster than population growth. Because roughly one-fourth of the world's population resides in South Asia and depends overwhelmingly on these food crops, the benefit to this region has been enormous.

The most recent change—one that is steeped in controversy—is the introduction of genetically modified crops. Genetically modified crops are those into which genes from unrelated species have been introduced. Such crops have the potential to greatly increase productivity. For example, cotton can be given a gene that makes it more resistant to herbicides and pesticides. When these chemical agents are applied to fields, weeds and pests are killed but the cotton plants are not. This has been controversial because of the alleged health effects for humans, potential environmental impacts, and disruption of current food production systems. This new technology is being introduced in a limited fashion, and the total environmental impact remains unknown and of concern to some.

OVERALL ECONOMIC STRUCTURE

To make economic statistics more meaningful, people often speak of the economy in terms of broad categories referred to as "sectors." There are four sectors—the primary, secondary, tertiary, and quaternary. The primary sector includes all economic activities that relate to the use of natural resources, such as farming, fishing, forestry, and mining. Secondary sector activities, which include manufacturing and construction, are those that add value to a product. When lumber extracted in the primary sector is used to build a table, the value of the product (the table) is greater than the value of the lumber itself. Tertiary sector activities are those that involve services such as wholesale, retail, medical care, and many other activities in which a service is performed. If you work in a restaurant, cut hair, or work for a financial services firm, you are employed in the service sector. The quaternary sector is composed of administrative activities, including working for the government or heading a company.

Economic sectors can be divided in another way. In the United States, most people work at jobs in which salary, social security, and other taxes are paid and the businesses are properly licensed by the government. This is called "formal employment." In other parts of the world, many people are employed casually (although this does not mean they work at a "casual" pace!). They oftentimes do not work for licensed firms or pay taxes. Such people are said to work in the "informal sector." Black market activities, those that are illegal or otherwise outside the law or regulation, are also in the informal category. This means that in cities such as Delhi, Mumbai, Dhaka, and Karachi, most people who sell goods on the street belong to the informal sector. In many countries, including those in South Asia, people who migrate to the city often are unable to find "regular jobs." They are forced to become involved in the informal economy, because working in the informal sector provides at least some income.

Many of the least-skilled rural-to-urban migrants find themselves working in the informal sector. These people often are unable to read and write, possess few technical skills, and have little in the way of material wealth. They may hawk foodstuffs from street corners, vend goods from street stalls, or even scavenge from landfills. Working from before dawn until dusk, they often sleep on the street itself. If they are fortunate enough to get a little ahead, they may send money to their families in the village or perhaps they invest in some building materials to build an illegal shanty in a slum. This way of living is not uncommon. In fact, half of Mumbai residents are slum dwellers and nearly half a million live on the streets.

There are two other ways of making economic statistics more meaningful. One is to interpret them in terms of jobs, or employment. A second way to make economic statistics meaningful is to speak of economic value in terms of gross domestic product, or GDP. This refers to the total value of goods and services produced by an economy. If one were to add up all the goods (cars, trucks, resources, and whatever else is extracted or manufactured) and services produced in one year, the resulting figure would be the country's or region's GDP. GDP is a rough measure of a country's overall wealth.

As noted previously, for thousands of years, most South Asians have tilled the soil. They have made their living from the land, working either for themselves or others, tending small plots to grow mostly basic food crops. This remains the case today, as the majority of Indians, Bangladeshis, and Nepalis grow crops of one sort or another. In Pakistan and Sri Lanka, the numbers are slightly lower, but the majority of people in each country remains tied to the land. Lacking machinery, quality seeds, and fertilizers and being plagued by a number of other problems, agriculture remains unproductive and inefficient. Thus, it generates little in per capita (per person) terms.

Even though most South Asians continue make their living from the land, the nonagricultural sectors of the economy are now of greatest importance in terms of wealth generated. In fact, agriculture continues to decline sharply relative to the other economic sectors. For example, in India, more than 60 percent of all workers are employed in agriculture, yet they

Although trends in Southeast Asia's labor force are beginning to shift from agriculture to manufacturing, services, and other predominantly urban sectors, there are still many signs of an agricultural society, such as this vegetable seller along the street in Rajasthan, India.

produce less than one-third of the country's GDP. In comparison, the primary sector in the United States, which includes agriculture, employs less than 3 percent of all workers.

Trends in South Asia's labor force are quite similar to the historical trends in other regions and countries of the world. Economic growth is accompanied by shifts of workers and output from agriculture to manufacturing, services, and other predominantly urban sectors. Particulars of this transition from agricultural to urban-based economies vary from country to country, but the basic trend remains. This change is so consistent that scientists who study developing economies call it a "sectoral shifts model." The model shows that a shift of workers out of agriculture is accompanied at first by a growth of the proportion of workers engaged in manufacturing. This is followed by a growth in service employment. In later stages of development, growth in the service sector continues as manufacturing employment declines and the number of people employed in agriculture begins to bottom out. Of course, these changes in industrial structure come with changes in numerous other social indicators. Life expectancy and literacy improve, as do economic indicators such as investment and personal income, in what is called the "development process." This process was a little different in South Asia, because the service sector grew sooner and faster than was predicted. Today, the service sector is the second-leading category of employment for most of South Asia. In Pakistan and Sri Lanka, however, it is the employer.

Following a brief stabilization period after independence came in 1947, India mimicked what was had been done in a number of developed countries, including the United Kingdom and the Soviet Union: It adopted an economic development strategy that involved a high degree of government involvement, regulation, and central planning. The idea was that the government, armed with technical expertise, funds, and good leadership, would guide investment, development in certain economic sectors, and economic development in certain poor regions. In implementing this government-led strategy, India used a series of "five-year plans" that specified the specific steps to be taken and goals to be reached. Certain industries, such as steelmaking, were targeted to be the backbone of the growing economy and were protected from outside competition. These protected industries were supplying what previously had been imported, thus the name "import substitution" for the policy. Import substitution served two purposes: First, it protected industries considered critical to long-term domestic economic development; second, in the aftermath of colonial domination, it helped many countries such as India work to free themselves from further commercial domination.

Economic growth during the period of central planning was steady but painfully slow. The benefit of the steady growth was that it provided stability to the Indian economy. It allowed for some national integration of the different regions and was aimed at improving life for the masses.

There were, however, many disadvantages. The population was growing at nearly the same rate as the economy, resulting in very small or nonexistent per capita gains. Protected industries that benefited from import substitution became inefficient because they lacked the incentives provided by outside competition. For example, without the threat of competition, Indian automobiles were notoriously unreliable, and designs were never changed. Indian cars of the 1970s looked much like those of the British cars of the 1940s, on which the designs were based. In addition, regulation became increasingly bureaucratic. Acquiring a business license often took months. This also led to corruption, as public servants often solicited bribes in order to supplement their meager paychecks.

In the 1980s, Indian economists, seeing the rapidly developing economies of first Japan and then the "Asian Tigers"—Korea, Singapore, Hong Kong, and Taiwan—began to question the economic development strategy they had chosen. Prime Minister Rajiv Gandhi realized that much of their growth was driven by foreign investment, free-market incentives, and export-oriented manufacturing strategies. He therefore decided to reform India's economy. Risking unbalanced growth and political uncertainly, Gandhi's successor, Narasimha Rao, further liberalized the economy in 1991 through privatizing some state-owned industries, deregulating industry, and allowing greater foreign investment.

Today, India's economy continues to improve as a result of the reforms. Its annual growth rate has exceeded 5 percent during most of the past decade. When compared to other large, developing economies, India trails only China's explosive advancement. This vibrant and rapid growth has lifted more than 100 million Indians out of poverty. It also has led to the emergence of both a wealthy elite and a burgeoning middle class of several hundred million. Consumerism is rampant, investors are optimistic, and the entrepreneurial spirit thrives in India's cities.

In 2005, India's overall economic production (GDP) is the world's twelfth largest. On a per capita basis, however, it amounts to the purchasing power equivalent of a little less than U.S. $3,000. This amount is meager when compared to developed countries such as the United States, with a per capita GDP of about $36,000. Today's Indian economy is dominated by the service sector, which provides about 50 percent of the GDP. The remainder is split almost evenly between the primary and secondary sectors. The secondary sector includes a variety of traditional craft industries based on local cultural traditions, available resources, and marketing possibilities. They include activities such as pottery, jewelry making, and carving, as well as silk weaving, cotton weaving, and even cigarette making. These household industries are in decline relative to the more modern manufacturing activities. Textiles and clothing are India's leading exports, although chemicals and engineered goods also are important. The United States is India's biggest trading partner, accounting for about 20 percent of both imports and exports.

India appears to have a bright future in the development and marketing of information technologies, especially software development. Indian software firms have gained a solid reputation for the high quality of their programs. In terms of global markets, they also benefit from low labor costs. In other technology areas, India has the same advantage in producing items of affordable quality.

One highly controversial economic area in which India is involved is the outsourcing of call centers and other office activities. Beginning in the late 1990s and more noticeably after 2000, many global companies relocated service call center activities from the United States to locations in Indian cities such

The noise inside a 24/7 customer call center crescendos to a climax with the noise of nearly 1,300 phone conversations. Simultaneously, agents working for nine U.S. Fortune 500 companies hawk credit cards, adjust phone bills, track package shipments, and advise clients on financial decisions.

as Mumbai, Bangalore, and Hyderabad. This was done because India offers a highly educated labor supply and very low rates for long-distance calls.

In terms of GDP, the economic structures of Bangladesh, Sri Lanka, and Pakistan are quite similar to that of India. Roughly half of each country's GDP comes from services and about 20 to 30 percent from the primary and secondary sectors. In Nepal, Afghanistan, and Bhutan, agriculture not only remains important for employment, but also is the leading economic sector in value.

In terms of per capita GDP purchasing power parity (PPP), Pakistan ($1,950) and Bangladesh ($1,550) are both poorer than India ($3,000), as are Nepal ($1,330) and Bhutan ($1,120). At $3,230 per capita, only Sri Lanka outranks India within the subcontinent. Again, comparison of these figures with the U.S. per capita GDP-PPP of about $36,000 places the region's relative poverty in perspective. Over the longer term, India is perhaps at an advantage economically because of its stable political base, economies of scale, and the relative quality of its postsecondary educational institutions.

Elsewhere in the region, political uncertainties threaten and undercut investment activities. Each country except India has seen potential economic progress retarded as a result of such uncertainty. Pakistan has suffered from ethnic violence and Islamic extremism; Tamil separatism has hindered economic growth in Sri Lanka; Maoist guerrillas plague Nepal; and Bangladesh has suffered under a series of unstable governments. These and other problems that contribute to instability have combined to discourage investment activity.

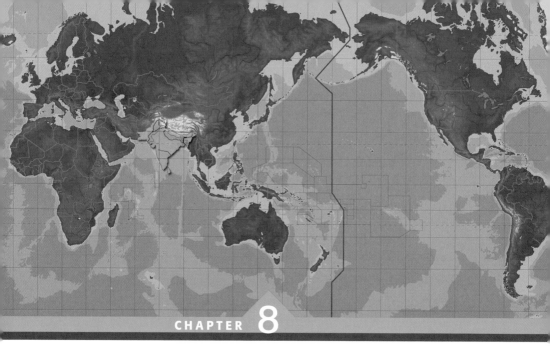

CHAPTER 8

Regional Contrasts

As a land of 22,000 dialects, more than half a dozen major religions, and a multitude of ethnic groups that is still steeped in local traditions, South Asia offers a panorama of landscapes. Dominating the scene today are the great urban centers. In addition, there are several regions of special character and interest.

THE GREAT CITIES

Colonial history played a large part in molding the subcontinent's megacities. Mumbai, Kolkata, Chennai, and Karachi all provided a base for transportation of goods to and from the region. Each was also an important British administrative center. New Delhi was not a port city but became the most prominent administrative center

These slum dwellings contrast sharply with the high-rise apartments (background) in the Bandra suburb of Mumbai, January 8, 2004.

in 1911, when the British transferred their political head-quarters there.

Today, these cities are growing too rapidly to adequately accommodate the influx of people from the countryside. Slums are common in all of these cities because there is simply not enough affordable housing. These slums are characterized by dilapidated housing, overcrowding, lack of ventilation, little or no sewage treatment, and lack of clean drinking water. A local term, *bustee*, is used for the word "slum" in many areas. Before 1970, most slums were simply bulldozed, but this policy of clearance simply relocated the problem to other areas of a city. Now, governments try to improve life within the slums. Public facilities are being upgraded, and slum dwellers are encouraged to take charge of improvement projects, often with appropriate government assistance.

Today, Mumbai is to India what both New York and Los Angeles are to the United States: It is both the "Wall Street" and "Hollywood" of India. The sprawling metropolis is the country's financial center and is home to much of India's motion picture and television industries. In fact, more movies are made in Mumbai each year than anywhere else in the world! It is a vibrant city full of opportunity. Projected to grow to 26 million people in the next decade, Mumbai soon will become the world's second-largest city. Despite its economic growth, 50 percent of Mumbai's residents live in slum conditions. Pavement dwellers, those who have no home and sleep on the streets each night, are estimated to number 250,000!

Before Mumbai occupied the top spot among South Asian cities, Kolkata was king. It grew tremendously after the British established a trading post and fort there in 1756. Until 1911, it was the center of the region's colonial government. With enormous population growth and location in a lowland area prone to flooding, it quickly acquired a reputation as one of the world's worst cities in which to live. Once plagued by malaria, cholera, and other tropical diseases, and with large number of homeless people, the city acquired a number of nicknames. None of these were complimentary: "City in a Swamp," "City of Pavement Dwellers," and "Cholera Capital of the World."

Delhi is India's capital city. Because of their strategic location, Delhi and ancient cities nearby were often the seats of power. Seventeen different sites in the local area have been excavated, and each of these cities were shown to have served, in turn, as the center of power in the region for most of the past 3,000 years. Delhi's location is so key to control of the Indo-Gangetic Plain that there is an old saying: "He who controls Delhi controls India."

The city has two components: Old Delhi and New Delhi. Old Delhi represents traditional cities of the region. It has traditional bazaar (market) areas and a complicated tangle of streets and byways. New Delhi was a planned city built in 1911 by the British to serve their needs. Unlike Old Delhi, it has wide streets laid out in geometric fashion. Today, it is home to the Indian government. Currently, Delhi is the fourteenth most populated city in the world and surely will climb up the ranks during coming years.

Karachi is Pakistan's largest city and most important trading center. Kidnapping, robbery, gang warfare, and organized crime are so prevalent that many people consider the city practically lawless. Add a recent wave of religion-based terrorism and one can understand why Karachi is now referred to as "the world's most dangerous city."

DIVERSE LANDSCAPES

Because of history and local culture, some places offer distinctive and special landscapes. Here is a sampling of those special attractions.

Goa is a tiny territory on India's west coast. Its special character results from a historical oddity. When the countries of the subcontinent became fully independent in 1947, there were some quirky exceptions. Until 1962, Goa remained a Portuguese colony! It was a remnant from the colonial past, having been negotiated away from the local Indian rulers by Portugal in 1510. Portugal expanded trading operations only slightly over the next several hundred years, until about 1800. Goa quietly functioned as a minor colony of a small European power, and no one paid it much attention. Finally, in 1961, the Indian army peacefully marched into the small territory and the Portuguese did not object.

A combination of its longtime political isolation and the unique influences of its Portuguese culture has given the region a culture that, by India's standards, is a bit "loose." It has earned a reputation as a place where traditional social rules are not as tight. Skirts are shorter, drug laws are largely ignored, and nude beaches attract bathers—and observers. Many Western tourists flocked here in the 1960s, and some still do, drawn by the aforementioned conditions, as well as the fantastic sand beaches and a local culture that offers a blend of Indian and Portuguese customs.

The lower elevations of the Himalayas offer a unique and inviting landscape that that is increasingly popular as a tourist destination. Trekking—taking long-distance walks in mountain areas—is particular popular and is especially important as a tourist activity in parts of North India and Nepal. Violence in Pakistan and Kashmir has frightened away tourists in those areas, even though they are ideal for such activities. Trekking is based out of the hill stations (discussed in Chapter 2), which are ideally located for trekking and mountain-climbing activities. Treks often take a week or even two to complete. People can make their own arrangements, hire others to coordinate arrangements, or hire others to serve as porters for their party.

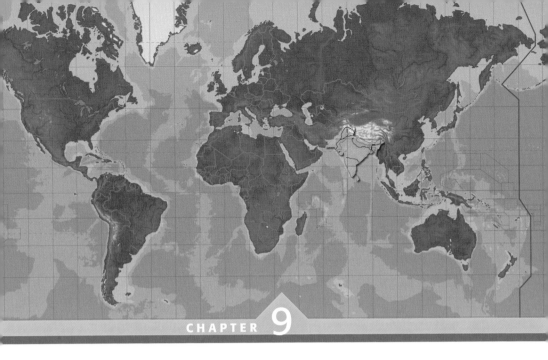

CHAPTER 9

South Asia
Looks Ahead

Although the countries of South Asia have experienced war, social strife, and poverty in the nearly 60 years since colonial rule ended, life for the masses has improved dramatically. If there is one common denominator in the region it is the persistence of hope.

In the face of this hope stand a number of challenges that threaten the political and economic stability that has been achieved. Here is a "top ten" list of the hurdles that South Asia faces. The ranking is subjective.

#10 ETHNIC VIOLENCE IN SRI LANKA

Conflict between the Sri Lankan government and Tamil separatists has plagued the country for more than a decade. Not only does it threaten lives in Sri Lanka, but it also may create opportunities for separatists in other parts of South Asia, particularly India. India's brief intervention in the late 1980s did nothing to solve the conflict; rather, it led to a Tamil terrorist suicide bombing that took Indian Prime Minister Rajiv Gandhi's life in 1991.

#9 THE INSTABILITY OF PAKISTAN

Pakistan has never experienced long-lasting civilian governance, and government control, even by the military, over Pakistan's territory has rarely been full and complete. It is believed that, in the remote frontier areas along the Afghanistan border, it is not Pakistani army soldiers but tribal militias who are in control. Rumors even say that the army needs permission from tribal leaders just to be allowed into these areas. This instability not only threatens social order in Pakistan, but also provides a haven for terrorists, including the remnants of Afghanistan's Taliban and Osama bin Laden.

#8 CASTE DIVISIONS IN INDIA

Caste divisions threaten and hinder India's progress. Discrimination against people of low caste, especially untouchables (*Dalits*), continues to be pervasive, particularly in rural environments. Hopefully, modernization and urbanization will slowly break the chains that bind people to discriminatory beliefs. Unfortunately, since India gained independence, when the caste system was outlawed, the chains have not loosened very much. The government has taken an active role by banning caste-based discrimination and by implementing a "reservation" system similar to affirmative action in the United States: A percentage of government jobs is guaranteed to those in certain lower-ranking castes. Many upper-caste people resent this program, and several young people have protested with self-immolation—setting themselves on fire. Sadly, it appears as though India and other countries in South Asia will suffer discrimination on the basis of caste, ethnicity, and religion for some time to come.

#7 STATUS OF WOMEN.

Women in South Asia continue to receive unequal treatment. This undermines economic development and undervalues the lives of hundreds of millions. Female fetuses are more often selectively aborted and, if born, females are more likely to die in the first year of life. As adults, women farmers are less likely to receive needed aid or loans and are generally treated with less respect. Perhaps the best indication of well-being is the sex ratio. This is the number of women for every 100 men. Ideally it should be roughly 100, yet in most of South Asia, it is woefully below that number. In some villages, the ratio is less than 70 women for every 100 men. This means that the females either were never born or died prematurely.

#6 COMMUNALISM

Religious strife threatens each nation and destroys thousands of lives each year. Conflict between religious groups erupts frequently, and with most people being either Muslim or Hindu, violence between these two groups is most common. The proximity of so many people of so many faiths provides a rich diversity but also leaves greater potential for conflict.

In recent years, some politicians have exploited religious antagonism. The city of Ayodhya was site of such politically driven religious conflict in 1992. A mob of Hindus, urged on by politicians, destroyed a nearly 400-year-old Islamic mosque. The site was holy to both Muslims and Hindus, and many people from each group resented control of the site by the other. In the violence that followed, several thousand people died. With the rise of Hindu nationalist political parties, more of such communal violence has occurred. With political parties based on religion, it is probable that leaders seeking greater public support for their parties (and faiths), will encourage further violence in a vicious and expanding cycle.

#5 POPULATION PRESSURES

A very large and growing population threatens the adequate provision of food and basic services to all of the population. The countries of South Asia have demonstrated an ability to feed their populations, but their economies have not consistently grown in a rapid manner. This leaves per capita incomes low, underemployment and unemployment high, and resources threadbare and overburdened. Fortunately, social and economic development, especially in India and Bangladesh, has led to a decline in birth rates and an increase in social well-being. In large areas of all countries in this region, population pressures threaten to overwhelm the ability to deal with social and economic problems.

#4 ENVIRONMENTAL DEGRADATION

A host of environmental problems has emerged on the subcontinent. Because of both population pressures and increased affluence, environmental quality is deteriorating. Cities are choked with smog levels that are among the world's worst. Clean drinking water is scarce and a valuable commodity in many locations. Throughout the region, endangered species are threatened with loss of habitat and overexploitation.

Water resources are being depleted and water quality is deteriorating because of agricultural and urban use. Irrigation is critical to agricultural prosperity, but overexploitation has left some soils waterlogged and others saline (too salty or with too many other minerals). In many cases, wells have been left dry as the water table has dropped. Water quality in cities is affected by the dumping of sewage and other wastes directly into rivers. Clean drinking water is not something that one can take for granted.

Urban environments are so deteriorated that respiratory ailments are common. Thick, heavy, dangerous smog blankets all of the largest cities. India's capital, Delhi, is particularly susceptible.

Many people in less-developed countries rely on wood for fuel. Deforestation for fuel and for the clearing of new agricultural land is now leading to erosion at a tremendous rate. This is especially true in steep-sloped areas such as Nepal. Deforestation has led to devastating landslides in that country and in other steep-sloped areas. Valuable agricultural soils also are rapidly being washed away in many areas.

Tangled together in a complicated knot are issues #3, #2, and #1. Each threatens peace on the subcontinent.

#3 KASHMIR

The passions stoked by the battle to control this region threaten to bring full-scale war and may also lead to an escalation of terrorist activities. With its rugged terrain, Muslim population, and tribal social organization, Kashmir is more like Afghanistan than like either India or Pakistan. Many of the tribal peoples of the region sympathize with the Taliban and Osama bin Laden's al Qaeda network. Some observers suspect that a link between the tribal peoples of Pakistan who shelter al Qaeda operatives and some tribal groups in Kashmir may exist. India claims that it was a suicide squad of Kashmiris with al Qaeda connections (and trained by Pakistan) that bombed and attempted to destroy India's legislative buildings in December 2001. This incident nearly brought India and Pakistan to war, as each country rapidly mobilized its military forces in the few days after the attack.

When independence came in 1947, Kashmir was a Hindu-ruled kingdom with an overwhelming majority of Muslims. Unlike most of the princely states, the maharaja of Kashmir hesitated for three months while trying to decide whether to join either India or Pakistan. He really wanted to remain independent,

Troops of the Border Security Force (BSF) patrol near the Line of Control (LOC) that divides Indian and Pakistani Kashmir at Ramgarh sector, December 27, 2001.

but controversially, and as a result of events that are still subject to debate, he opted to join India. Some contend that Pakistan urged rebel tribesmen to revolt; others say that conflict erupted when India occupied the region with its troops. When his power was threatened, the maharaja opted to join India. This triggered war between Pakistan and India and resulted in Pakistan occupying one-third of the region and India most of the rest. China controls a small bit, too, and claims even more of this remote and beautiful mountain territory.

Since that time, both India and Pakistan have laid claim to Kashmir. In the three wars fought between the two countries, Kashmir was a key objective each time. Some Kashmiris even agitate to be independent from both Pakistan and India. Today, a "line of control" divides the region into the parts that are occupied by Pakistan and those held by India. Although these countries are not officially at war at this time, troops on each side occasionally fire at one another. This may be thought of as a "hot spot in a cold war." Some parts along this line of control are at such high elevations (18,000 feet) that troops can only be sent in three-month rotations.

What will be the eventual "solution" for Kashmir? No one can say; however, everyone can say that more blood will be spilled and lives destroyed before the conflict is resolved. Meanwhile, the region continues to serve as hotbed of violence and source of terrorists.

#2 NUCLEAR PROLIFERATION

In 1998, India conducted nuclear weapons tests. Pakistan responded with its own tests shortly thereafter. Each country was serving notice to the other that it had nuclear military capability. The world feared that this posturing could lead to open nuclear conflict. Such a conflict would leave millions dead and both countries in ruins. It would also spark further conflict.

#1 WAR BETWEEN INDIA AND PAKISTAN

Since South Asia became independent, three wars between these nations have shattered peace on the subcontinent. In part because of religious factors, these two countries have an intense dislike for and rivalry with each other. In 1948, a year after South Asia gained independence, military conflict was triggered by the conflict over Kashmir. A second war was fought over Kashmir in 1965. Pakistan thought it could gain the advantage by co-opting local resistance, but the war largely resulted in a continuation of the stalemate. A third war was fought in 1971–1972 as a result of the civil war between the future Bangladesh and what remained as Pakistan. India stepped into the conflict when refugees flooded into the country and when Bangladeshi guerrilla fighters began to base operations in India.

A cold war situation has held since that time, although scattered combat has occurred on a limited basis in Kashmir.

These countries continue their intense rivalry. When sporting events such as cricket matches occur between Indian and Pakistani teams, they become a matter of national pride. Viewers are glued to their television sets and listeners to their radios. It is almost as if war is being fought on the athletic field instead of the field of combat. Hopefully, the conflict will remain confined to sports venues. An all-out war that included the use of nuclear weapons would likely result in millions of deaths. More than any other threat, this one is most likely to fracture and destroy lives in South Asia.

Of all the countries of South Asia, India is the closest to achieving long-term economic growth, political stability, and widespread human well-being. The country has worked hard to establish and maintain a democratic framework. Its founders recognized that a stable and fair political setting would provide the social order necessary to build a prosperous and wealthy nation. Even if this process takes a painfully long time, it is the foundation that *must* be laid. The countries that will have the most difficulty in becoming prosperous are those with the weakest democratic traditions. Pakistan is believed to face the most difficult future; it must wrestle with all of the challenges without the political stability necessary for the job.

South Asia, anchored by India, has the opportunity to follow rapidly developing China in economic growth. If it is able to maintain a fair, stable, democratic government it may surpass China's achievements during the twenty-first century. The region is on the cusp of long-term economic growth and widespread well-being. Let us hope that the people of South Asia achieve that dream.

Before 3000 B.C.	The earliest peoples inhabit South Asia; their cultural legacy remains in the tribal peoples of today.
3000 B.C.	The earliest civilizations arise in Indus Valley with the establishment of cities Harappa and Mohenjo-daro.
1500 B.C.	Indus Valley civilizations disappear, perhaps in response to environmental change or invasion by the Aryans; the earliest Aryans begin to arrive from southwest and central Asia and slowly either subjugate or push the Dravidian peoples farther south; Hinduism becomes the dominant religion over the next 1,000 or so years.
322–150 B.C.	The Mauryan Empire is established, bringing uniform political and administrative control to much of the region; this stability allows the economy to flourish and cultural unity to be established; the reign of Ashoka (269–232 B.C.), characterized by his endorsement of Buddhism as the state religion, is seen as the high point of this empire.
A.D. 320–550	The rise of the Gupta Empire brings a second long period of stability across much of South Asia; advancements and innovations occur in art, architecture, law, literature, science, and trade.
711	Muslims invade what is present-day Pakistan; Islam is introduced to South Asia.
1206	The earliest Islamic occupation of territory in the region by invasion is marked by Turko-Afghan conquest of Delhi.
1498	The first appearance of Europeans in the region occurs with Vasco da Gama's visit to the southern tip of present-day India.
1502	The Portuguese establish a trading post in Goa on the west coast of the Deccan Peninsula; Goa remains a colony of Portugal until 1962.
1526	Islamic invasions culminate in the conquest of Delhi by the Moguls, who displace the weaker Muslim rulers; the Moguls work to consolidate their control over most of the region in the two centuries that follow; the imposition of Islam on much of the population makes it the second-leading faith.
1556–1605	The zenith of Mogul rule occurs with the administration of Akbar the Great; he attempts to reconcile Muslim–Hindu differences while establishing economic and political control and stability.

1630–1653	Emperor Shah Jahan has the Taj Mahal built; this tomb to one of his beloved wives best represents the influence of Islamic architecture on India and other parts of region.
1765	The British begin to cement their occupation with military victories and administration of parts of eastern India; their presence most strongly emanates from the "Presidency Towns" of Kolkata (then Calcutta), Mumbai (then Bombay) and Madras (now Chennai); all trade is controlled by British East India Company.
1857	The first "war of independence" occurs, and the British prevail; however, the trade monopoly and administration of the East India Company ends, and direct British rule begins; this coincides with trade moving from mercantile based to industrial based, with India sending increasing amounts of raw materials to Britain for manufacturing.
1930	Gandhi protests the salt tax by marching to the sea to gather salt.
1947	On August 15, independence arrives for India and Pakistan.
1948	Sri Lanka (then called Ceylon) gains independence; India and Pakistan battle over Kashmir.
1965	India and Pakistan battle over Kashmir.
1968	The Maldives become independent.
1971	East and West Pakistan fight a civil war with intervention from India; this leads to independence for East Pakistan, which is now called Bangladesh.
1975–1989	Bangladesh is governed by martial law.
1977–present	Separatist "Tamil Tigers" (a militant Hindu group) rebel in Sri Lanka.
1984	Indian Prime Minister Indira Gandhi is assassinated by her Sikh bodyguards in retaliation for her ordering the Sikh's Golden Temple to be stormed by the military.
1991	Indian Prime Minister Rajiv Gandhi is assassinated.
2000–present	Nepal is plagued by Maoist (Communist) insurgency; India and Pakistan conduct missile and nuclear weapons tests
2001	The Nepalese royal family is killed by Crown Prince Dipendra, who then commits suicide.

Benhart, John S., and C. Robert Scull. *Regions of the World Today*. 3rd ed. Dubuque, IA: Kendall/Hunt Publishing, 1998.

Dutt, Ashok K., and M. Margaret Geib. *Atlas of South Asia: A Geographic Analysis by Countries*. New Delhi: Oxford & IBH Publishing, 1998.

Chapman, Graham P. *Geopolitics of South Asia: From Early Empires to India, Pakistan and Bangladesh*. Aldershot, Hampshire, UK: Ashgate Publishing, 2000.

Farmer, B.H. *An Introduction to South Asia*. 2nd ed. New York: Routledge, 1993.

Noble, Allen G., and Ashok K. Dutt, eds. *India: Cultural Patterns and Processes*. Boulder, CO: Westview Press, 1982.

Shurmer-Smith, Pamela. *India: Globalization and Change*. London: Arnold, 2000.

Spate, O.H.K., and T.A. Learmonth. *India and Pakistan: Land, People and Economy*. 4th ed. London: Methuen, 1972.

Tirtha, Ranjit. *Society and Development in Contemporary India: Geographical Perspectives*. Detroit, MI: Harlo Press, 1980.

Wolpert, Stanley. *A New History of India*. 4th ed. New York: Oxford University Press, 1993.

BOOKS

Crompton, Samuel Willard. *Pakistan (Modern World Nations)*. Philadelphia: Chelsea House Publishers, 2003.

Forster, E.M. *A Passage to India* (Everyman's Library). New York: Alfred A. Knopf, 1992. First published 1924.

LaPierre, Dominick. *City of Joy*. Garden City, NY: Doubleday, 1985.

Naipul, V.S. *An Area of Darkness: A Discovery of India*. New York: Vintage Books, 2002. Originally published in 1964.

Naipul, V.S. *India: A Million Mutinies Now*. New York: Viking, 1991.

Narayan, R.K. *Malgudi Days*. New York: Penguin Group, 1995. Originally published in 1982.

Phillips, Douglas A., and Charles F. Gritzner. *India (Modern World Nations)*. Philadelphia: Chelsea House Publishing, 2003.

Roy, Arundhati. *The God of Small Things*. New York: Harper Perennial, 1998.

Thapar, Romila. *History of India 1*. New York: Penguin Books, 1996.

Theroux, Paul. *The Great Railway Bazaar*. New York: Penguin Books, 1995.

WEBSITES

Asian Studies WWW Virtual Library
http://coombs.anu.edu.au/WWWVL-AsianStudies.html
This is an academic-based Website for general Asian studies.

Bangladesh, the Government of
http://www.bangladeshgov.org
This is the official site for the government of Bangladesh.

Bangladesh WWW Virtual Library
http://asnic.utexas.edu/asnic/countries/bangla/
This academic-based Website has links that relate to Bangladesh.

CIA World Factbook
http://www.cia.gov/cia/publications/factbook/index.html
This CIA site is a current source of basic characteristics and statistics for countries around the world, including those in South Asia.

The Government of India
http://indiaimage.nic.in/
This is the official Website for the government of India.

WEBSITES (continued)

Incredible! India
http://www.india-tourism.com/
This is a government India tourism site.

India WWW Virtual Library
http://www.india.com.ar/

This academic-based Website has links that relate to India.
Lonely Planet
http://www.lonelyplanet.com/
This travel guide Website may serve as an enjoyable and informative introduction to South Asia.

Pakistan Tourism Development Corporation
http://www.tourism.gov.pk/
This is a government-sponsored Website for Pakistan.

Pakistan Virtual Library
http://www.clas.ufl.edu/users/gthursby/pak/
This is an academic-based informational Website.

SARAI—South Asian Resource Access on the Internet
http://www.columbia.edu/cu/lweb/indiv/southasia/cuvl/
This academic-based Website's general focus is South Asia.

Times of India
http://timesofindia.indiatimes.com/
This is one of India's leading English-language newspapers.

Virtual Bangladesh
http://www.virtualbangladesh.com/
This Web site is a profile of Bangladesh.

page:

2: Zuma Press/New Millennium Images
5: © Mapping Specialists, Ltd.
10: KRT/New Millennium Images
12: © Mapping Specialists, Ltd.
14: Reuters/Amit Dave/New Millennium Images
19: New Millennium Images
24: © Diego Lexama Orezzoli/CORBIS
29: New Millennium Images
36: KRT/New Millennium Images
38: © Mapping Specialists, Ltd.
42: AFP/New Millennium Images
49: KRT/New Millennium Images
51: KRT/New Millennium Images

56: AFP/New Millennium Images
62: Associated Press, AP/Max Desfor
65: Associated Press, AP
68: Associated Press, AP/HO
72: Reuters/New Millennium Images
75: KRT/New Millennium Images
80: © Mapping Specialists, Ltd.
82: AFP/New Millennium Images
86: KRT/New Millennium Images
90: KRT/New Millennium Images
93: KRT/New Millennium Images
102: AFP/New Millennium Images
Cover: Associated Press, AP

JOHN S. BENHART has been Professor and Chair of the Geography - Earth Science Department at Shippensburg University of Pennsylvania over the past 30 plus years. During his tenure at Shippensburg University, he has served as Dean of the College of Arts and Sciences and Dean of Admissions. He has contributed extensively to geographic education through his leadership efforts in the National Council for Geographic Education (NCGE), the Pennsylvania Geographical Society (PGS), and the Regional Development and Planning Specialty Group of the Association of American Geographers (AAG). Dr. Benhart's research and teaching interests include world environments, environmental land use planning, Europe, and Asia. In October 2000 he was honored with the Distinguished Teaching Award from the NCGE and in 1995 he received the Pennsylvania Geographic Society's Distinguished Geographer Award. Dr. Benhart is entering his fifth decade of university teaching, research, and service.

GEORGE POMEROY is associate professor of geography at Shippensburg University of Pennsylvania. His research interests are urban geography, regional development and planning, and Asia. He focuses in particular on urbanization in India and China.

CHARLES F. ("FRITZ") GRITZNER is Distinguished Professor of Geography at South Dakota University in Brookings. He is now in his fifth decade of college teaching and research. During his career, he has taught more than 60 different courses, spanning the fields of physical, cultural, and regional geography. In addition to his teaching, he enjoys writing, working with teachers, and sharing his love for geography with students. As consulting editor for the MODERN WORLD NATIONS series, he has a wonderful opportunity to combine each of these "hobbies." Fritz has served as both President and Executive Director of the National Council for Geographic Education and has received the Council's highest honor, the George J. Miller Award for Distinguished Service. In March 2004, he won the Distinguished Teaching award from the American Association of Geographers at their annual meeting held in Philadelphia.